A LIFE FOR A LIFE

Life Imprisonment: America's Other Death Penalty

James A. Paluch, Jr.

Edited by

Thomas J. Bernard
Pennsylvania State University

Robert Johnson
American University

Roxbury Publishing Company
Los Angeles, California

Library of Congress Cataloging-in-Publication Data

Paluch, James A., Jr. 1971–
A life for a life / James A. Paluch, Jr.; Thomas Bernard, Robert
Johnson (eds.).
    p. cm.
Includes bibliographical references.
ISBN 1-931719-37-3
    1. Paluch, James A., Jr. 1971– . 2. Prisoners—Pennsylvania—
Biography. 3. Prisoners—Pennsylvania—Social conditions.
I. Bernard, Thomas 1945– II. Johnson, Robert, 1948– III. Title.

HV9468.P35P38 2004
365'.44'092—dc21
[B]   2003043188
                                                                  CIP

A LIFE FOR A LIFE: LIFE IMPRISONMENT: AMERICA'S OTHER
DEATH PENALTY

Publisher: Claude Teweles
Managing Editor: Dawn VanDercreek
Project and Copy Editor: Anton Diether
Production Editor: Jim Ballinger
Production Assistant: Joshua Levine
Proofreader: Amy C. Quick
Cover Design: Marnie Kenney
Typography: Abe Hendin, prepress@yourspeed.com

Printed on acid-free paper in the United States of America. This book
meets the standards of recycling of the Environmental Protection Agency.

ISBN 1-931719-37-3

ROXBURY PUBLISHING COMPANY
P.O. Box 491044
Los Angeles, California 90049-9044
Voice: (310) 473-3312 • Fax: (310) 473-4490
Email: roxbury@roxbury.net
Website: www.roxbury.net

Dedication

This book is dedicated to
YAHWEH
(Who created me in His image)

and to

James A. Paluch, Sr.
Anita L. Paluch
(who procreated me in theirs)

and to

the memory of all
those who have lost their
lives to senseless
acts of criminal homicide,
both living and dead.

"In your struggle for Justice,
let your oppressor know that
you're not attempting to
defeat or humiliate him, or
to even pay him back for the
injustices that he has heaped
upon you. Let him know
that you are merely seeking
justice for him as well
as yourself."

—Dr. Martin Luther King, Jr.

Contents

Foreword

Thomas J. Bernard
Pennsylvania State University

In December of 1999, James A. "Bof" Paluch, Jr., wrote me a letter in which he stated: "I am interested in writing a book about myself and the experience of being a lifer in Pennsylvania." After some correspondence between us, I drove out to SCI-Rockview, where Mr. Paluch was housed, and we met in the visiting room for several hours. During that meeting, I outlined my goals and conditions for working with him on such a project.

My primary goal, related to my role as an educator, was neither to attack nor defend prisons, but to accurately describe them. I wanted this book to be a fair, honest, and truthful depiction of prisons and prison life. I believe that it is important for students and the American public to learn what prisons are really like, because such an enormous number of people are locked up inside them.

By the end of 2001, over 1.3 million people were housed in prisons across the United States, which is about 470 prisoners for every 100,000 people in the nation's population. By contrast, in 1990, there were 292 prisoners for every 100,000 people; in the mid-1960s, there were fewer than 100 for every 100,000. Prior to 1960, the incarceration rate in the United States had never exceeded 110 prisoners per 100,000 people in the population. The era of our "get tough" policy has led to massive increases in prison populations.

Besides people in prison, over 600,000 more people are incarcerated in jails and over 100,000 more are locked up in juvenile facilities. At the end of 2001, over 2.1 million people were locked up in prisons, jails, and juvenile facilities in the United States. This results in a total incarceration rate of approximately 710 incarcerated people for every 100,000 people in the population.

This is the highest incarceration rate in the entire world (Russia is in second place with 628). Other Western industrialized countries typically have incarceration rates of somewhere around 100 per 100,000. For example, Canada has an incarceration rate of 102 per 100,000 and England has 139 per 100,000. On the other hand, Iceland has only 35 incarcerated people for every 100,000 people in their population.

Incarceration is one part of the total correctional system, which also includes probation and parole. At the end of 2001, 6.6 million people were under some form of correctional supervision in the United States. This is more than 3 percent of the entire population of the United States, a figure that I find astounding. In 1980, by contrast, 1.1 percent of the population was under some form of correctional supervision.

In our meeting three years ago in Rockview's visiting room, Mr. Paluch stated that he was interested in making policy recommendations about incarceration in his book, such as allowing life-sentenced inmates to be considered for parole. I was willing to include such recommendations, as long as the primary focus of the book remained on the honest and accurate description of prison life, thus allowing readers to draw their own conclusions about incarceration policies.

I emphasized in that meeting that the views expressed in the book would be Mr. Paluch's views, not mine. This is not to suggest that I disagree with his views. The fact is, I have never been a prisoner, never worked in a prison, nor have I ever focused on prisons in my academic career. Thus my views on prisons would not be very interesting to readers.

Mr. Paluch, on the other hand, has been a prisoner for over 13 years and thus has a great deal of knowledge and experience of prison life. Of course, readers should keep in mind that this book is written by a prisoner, therefore presented from a prisoner's point of view. A book written by a prison superintendent, for example, would obviously present a point of view quite different from that of an inmate.

I believe that prisons are enormously complex phenomena and that they are best understood by being seen from several points of view. One of those points of view, I firmly believe, should be the prisoner's.

In my opinion, this book is an honest attempt by a prisoner to speak honestly about prisons. Mr. Paluch worked very long and hard to be as fair and accurate as possible while speaking the truth about prison life as he sees it. As such, I believe that this book makes a valuable contribution to prison literature and that it will fulfill my goal of educating students and all Americans about America's prisons.

Acknowledgments

During the three years I worked with him, Mr. Paluch mailed me approximately 1,000 pages of material, all of which was either typed or handwritten and most of which came in envelopes with six or fewer pages. Christine Van Asten thoughtfully read all this material, made initial recommendations about which material to include in the book, and proposed an overall organizational framework for that material. Her work is strongly reflected in the final product. A. Dakari Alexander then performed the difficult and time-consuming task of putting the typed and handwritten material into a computerized form. He also did some initial editing of that material. I would like to thank these two hardworking individuals, without whose help this book could not have been completed. Of course, the views expressed in this book are solely those of the author, James A. Paluch, Jr. ✦

Author's Acknowledgments and Prologue

James A. Paluch, Jr.

Thomas J. Bernard, Ph.D., of the Pennsylvania State University is a *majestic* person. He served as the main editor of this book, and without his scholarly wisdom and willingness to assist me in giving a voice to Pennsylvania's lifers, the journey you are about to take would most likely never have happened. He believed in me when others did not, and was inclined to give me the opportunity to make a contribution to a society that has traditionally given up on its incarcerated citizens. For this, I am truly appreciative.

I am also indebted to Robert Johnson of the American University as co-editor of this project. His keen insights concerning the studies on capital punishment and life imprisonment as death penalties have given *A Life for a Life* a very special touch.

Very special appreciation is extended to Roxbury Publishing Company, namely, Claude Teweles, who has ventured to ensure that the voice of prisoners are heard. Likewise, I am appreciative to the following persons who contributed to this book: Jim Ballinger (Roxbury), Anton Diether of Polar Pictures, Jeffrey M. Hoelzel (a loyal brother), Dianna L. Hollis, Joyce Upchurch, and James A. Paluch, Sr.

To Ernest D. Preate, Jr., our lawyer. Lobbyist, advocate, friend and brother: your kindness and compassion are a strength that others would do well to emulate.

It would be an injustice not to mention the names of those individuals who work behind the scenes in support of the parole for lifers movement and for the much-needed criminal justice reforms in Pennsylvania: William M. DiMascio (Pennsylvania Prison Society), Dr. John Rush and Tom Zeager (Justice & Mercy, Inc.), Joan Gauker (Graterfriends, Inc.), Mr. and Mrs. George and Nancy McVaugh, and to all the volunteers too numerous to mention, especially at PA CURE. Angus Love, Esq., Samuel C. Stretton, Esq., David Rudovsky, Esq., Mitchell S. Strutin, Esq., James C. Lanshe, Sr., Esq., Carol (Bithyah) Strick, Dr. Pierre Duterte, Doret Kollerer (*The Justice Xpress*), Jim Campbell, Dr. Julia Hall (Drexel University), Dr. Julian Heicklen (Pennsylvania State University), Dr. Howard Zehr (Eastern Mennonite University), Jane Crosby, Harriet Kaylor, Susan Quinn, Rosemary Moran, Martin McIntyre, Big "V," Tuvia Abramson (PSU Hillel), Rita Foderaro, Marie Hamilton (CentrePeace, Inc.), Paul Vault, the Honorable Rabbi Lewis E. Bogage, James O. Smith, Sandra L. Grejdus, Brenda Fox, Tammy Potter, Veronica Phillips, Joseph D. Lehman, Harvey Bell, and Joan Ober. I also wish to thank Caryl Clarke (*York Daily Record*) and Nancy Eshelman (*Harrisburg Patriot-News*) for their excellence in journalism. Amongst all the friends of lifers we will sadly miss three special family members: Lois A. Williamson (d. 1995), Representative David P. Richardson (d. 1995), and Robert A. Preate (d. 2002). May Yahweh bless all of you.

There are some Pennsylvania legislators who also need to who also need to be praised for their efforts to represent a class of people who have no representation, administering the concept of equal justice under the law: Andrew J. Carn, Harold James, Edward Helfrick, Allen Kukovich, Ralph Acosta, Stewart J. Greenleaf, Thomas Armstrong, and the man who began this movement—Louis C. Johanson. We hope that in the future there will be many more legislators to esteem.

Lastly, I wish to thank all my fellow lifers in Pennsylvania who I have met throughout these past 13 years, who have made positive contributions not only in their own lives, but in the lives of others, and who have remained steadfast as leaders in the struggle, especially to: Jon E. Yount, Preston B. Pfeifley, Michael P. Small, Harry Twiggs, Cyd Charisse Berger, Mark "Wiz" Robinson, James Garrett, Eric Decker, Charles "Zeke" Goldblum, Doug Hollis, Janet Martin, Patricia Rorrer, and many others who have meritoriously earned their opportunity for redemption.

As author, I feel the need to let the reader know that there is actually more to this book than what you are about to read. For instance, difficult decisions were made to exclude very valuable information such as inmate employment, the success stories of those lifers who had their sentences commuted to parole, the unique experience of female lifers, the history of life imprisonment in Pennsylvania, and the many horror stories of injustice that frames the history of the Pennsylvania Department of Corrections. There was just so much that needed to be said, but few precious pages to tell it on. My hope is that the reader will end this book with a more profound understanding of what prison life is about, and what it does to people.

At the time Roxbury Publishing Company agreed to publish this book, I was issued a misconduct report at SCI-Rockview for an assault on another inmate which never happened. The hearing examiner did not allow me to question the reporting staff member, nor was I allowed to call any witnesses on my behalf. I was punished unfairly, in my opinion, and I believe this came about as a result of my continued efforts to have my voice heard. After serving four months in solitary confinement, I was transferred to SCI-Houtzdale, farther away from home.

Such is my life.

Now, are you ready to listen?

—James A. Paluch, Jr.
SCI-Houtzdale

Preface to Instructors

Robert Johnson
American University

This book arrived in dribs and drabs, some entries handwritten, others typed, a story here, a key observation there. Over a three-year period, some 800 pages of material enclosed within six-page letters wended their way to freedom. Much like life itself, it took some effort to get the story straight. As the primary editor, Tom Bernard had the task of sculpting this raw material into a form that respected the flow of ideas and events conveyed by James Paluch, Jr., yet gave them a recognizable structure to outsiders who know prison only from a distance. This Bernard did admirably. Through his deft selection and editing, Bernard took the lead in producing a text that remains close to the world in which Paluch lives and allows the reader to readily enter that world. We recommend using the book for just that end—to introduce students to the prison world as a living environment, a place where days unfold and lives, sometimes entire lives, run their course.

Paluch's book offers us a road map of prison life. In my experience, students and colleagues can readily connect with his personal journey. We all live and work in environments that comprise special worlds for us. In a fair number of cases, those environments are set apart from the world at large. This is certainly true of many universities and corporations as well. Goffman (1961) once called these settings "total institutions," which included schools (especially boarding schools), the military, mental hospitals, and prisons. Institutions are arguably less total than they once were, but the concept still resonates. Many students in college should know something about living in a total institution, which they call a dorm. That knowledge can be used to build a bridge to the world of prison and to help students empathize with the incarcerated.

The key to using this book in class is to focus on that need for empathy. Students who want to understand prison need to open themselves up to the prison experience as it exists in the real world, rather than as they imagine it to be. Empathy means putting yourself in Paluch's shoes, walking a mile in his prison yard, settling in for an evening in his cell, chatting with his neighbors, watching out for predators who might well be watching you. The best way to promote empathy is to have students select quotations from the text that they wish to share with the class. They then read one of their selections out loud in class, noting briefly why they made that selection. Others are invited to comment or respond with a quotation of their own. Each student should read at least one quotation in each class, if the size of the class allows it. This format will clarify what the students find important and guide the discussion toward topics that matter to them.

The selection and reading of quotations from the text should also lead to insight—the application of knowledge to one's own life. Poignant stories and moving poems found in abundance in this book often breach the walls that separate citizens and convicts. Ideology gives way to intimacy, making it harder to fear or hate someone you know something about as a person, or to rely on stereotypes when you know better. Humanism is one thing, but it is quite another to feel a connection to someone ostensibly quite different from yourself.

This book also highlights the interplay of theory and practice. Theoretical concepts like prisonization, institutionalization, community, routine, power, and even the nature of modern punishment itself have concrete referents in this book. These concepts will come alive for students when they reach out and enter the life and experiences of James Paluch, Jr., a man serving a life sentence in prison with no hope of parole.

Source

Goffman, Erving. (1961). *Asylums.* Garden City, NY: Anchor Books. ✦

Introduction

Robert Johnson
American University

Life in Prison

The lure of books about prison is the prospect of a bird's eye view of life behind bars. Readers want to feel as if they have been there, seeing and feeling this alien, often frightening world that is reserved only for felons—people whom we imagine as very different from ordinary folk.

James A. Paluch, Jr.'s *A Life for a Life* gives a superbly detailed account of the daily realities of prison life in its mundane essentials, showing us how ordinary the people who inhabit this world really are. Paluch walks us through a complicated, sometimes treacherous culture behind bars, a place where manipulation and deception often rule. By the end of his book, readers should have gained considerable knowledge about prison as an institution and as a social world. They may very well question and reevaluate whether our prisons in their present condition should hold substantial numbers of offenders for the rest of their natural lives. To move readers to this point would be an achievement in these conservative times, for which Paluch should be deservedly proud.

Paluch is a meticulous writer who chronicles every detail of his world in clear, engaging prose. His scrupulous attention to everyday prison life may surprise readers who expect angry tales of abuse or political and ideological beefs with the world at large—not the author's daily accounts on the sanitary state of cells, the noise pollution in cell blocks, or the nature of meals and dinnerware in the mess hall. Paluch does report on some troubling abuses, but first and foremost he focuses on living conditions in his world as would a thoughtful, diligent anthropologist. When he relates an injustice, the very detail with which he conveys the situation adds credibility to his words.

From the outset, we are invited into Paluch's cell and treated to a thorough description of the compact world that frames his and every inmate's daily existence. He recounts a brief exchange that introduces him as a seasoned veteran of prison, an "o'head" (short for "old head"), a guide with valuable experience, even wisdom, in the ways of prison life. Yet he is only 32 years old, facing a lifetime of prison with perhaps 40 or 50 more years ahead of him. As we explore his world with him, the prospect of life imprisonment without the possibility of parole may seem so harsh as to be almost impossible to fathom.

Paluch did not enter prison as a seasoned convict, of course. Like many before and after him, he spent a long time coming to grips with the extraordinary sanctions imposed on him. He began as a scared youth of 19, facing a murder charge and confined to a jailhouse setting that bore all the earmarks of a dungeon. His world was turned upside down, with violence and despair now permeating his daily existence. In a short time, a fellow prisoner committed suicide, gangs of inmates fought savagely without interference by officers, and a stranger spat in his face for no apparent reason. His mother died soon after his confinement, but he could not attend her funeral. In nine months, he dropped 70 pounds from his 200-pound frame. As he coped with cockroaches and bad food, lonely and helpless, his life was falling apart at the seams.

After the testimony of witnesses, including his girlfriend, Paluch's fate was sealed in court. He was convicted of premeditated murder. Escaping the death penalty by the decision of 12 members of a jury, he was sentenced to life imprisonment without parole, a *living* death.

He next entered the menacing world of prison, gripped with understandable fears. He was as young as most college students reading this text, unschooled in street violence, concerned about rape, and terrified that he may die behind bars. He met an assortment of cellmates during his first days, none reassuring, and found himself with a man who threatened to kill him if he didn't vacate the cell. He faked a suicide to get reassigned and thus started his time in a mental health unit. One theme of this book is that the entire prison can be viewed as a kind of mental health unit where destructive, even crazy, behavior often prevails.

The author then takes us on a guided tour of a typical prison. We learn the routine, smell the smells, and shudder at the constant noise and lack of privacy. Prison is a place of pervasive discomfort and endless anxiety. We know that prisons are dangerous, but Paluch has a way of bringing this simple fact home by showing how fear shapes daily life. To be involved in a fight, for example, means that one is usually on one's own, as prison guards are too outnumbered to intervene. Paluch and most inmates never leave their cells without securing them with combination locks, unnerving testimony to the fact that a prisoner must lock his own cell to protect his property. Yet, a cell-door lock can be an illusory barrier to violence, as we read later how Paluch's cell was firebombed by an unknown arsonist. Had he been in his cell at the time, he would have been incinerated.

Paluch's book offers fresh insights into the concept that prisons are, first and foremost, living environments (see Toch 1992; Johnson 2002). Whatever purpose one may ascribe to these institutions, inmates have to live in them and get through each day as best as they can. They must forge a life behind bars, which means they must sleep, eat, bathe, shop, work, and play in the confines of the prison. As an example, Paluch introduces the mess hall, describing the layout and, more compellingly, the small portions of unappetizing food. We learn that unless a prisoner can secure money from outside, he must live with hunger as a constant companion; a stark contrast to the preconceived notion that prisoners live leisurely on "three hots and a cot," i.e., free food and housing. Paluch also points out the prevalence of such contagious diseases as hepatitis, impressing upon us that dining in an unsanitary mess hall can be a precarious experience.

To live decently in prison, inmates must get along with others, economize on limited budgets, and constantly improvise. They must maintain their health and sometimes do their own laundry to ensure clean clothes. They must negotiate such dangerous settings as understaffed prison yards and overcrowded showers. They must endure cold winter nights in badly heated cells and long days of endless lines, checkpoints, and bureaucratic red tape, even when they are in dire need of medical treatment. A call for emergency medical help outside of normal working hours can be a life-threatening battle for a prisoner, let alone having his medical needs met with concern. Prison is a lonely enough place to live in, but an even lonelier place in which to become seriously ill.

Life in prison is a litany of deprivations, a point made clear by Gresham Sykes in his classic text, *The Society of Captives* (Sykes 1958). Prisoners must go without many creature comforts and make do without heterosexual relations, including close physical contact with loved ones during visiting hours. Paluch argues for conjugal visits on the grounds that sex is a natural human necessity, and that its absence promotes homosexuality and harms marriages, ultimately even society itself. Readers will no doubt debate this, but the author's arguments may help them to consider how much deprivation is necessary, let alone humane, for punishments that last an entire lifetime. In the reality of prison, the only sexual alternatives for inmates are abstinence, masturbation, homosexuality, or sex with prison staff members of the opposite sex.

Prisons are run as a caste system separating inmates and staff. Meaningful contact across caste lines is limited, both groups in a sense imprisoned by their official roles (Lombardo 1989). Prisoner-staff relations can be cordial and even friendly, but trust and friendship are rare. Manipulation is a constant threat. To emphasize this point, Paluch describes how the "game" or "hustle" is endemic in prisons, inmates conning one another and staff members. At the same time, officers use their authority to manipulate and control inmates, sometimes issuing bogus misconduct reports that can ruin a prisoner's record, even costing him his chance for parole.

Both inmates and staff are in precarious positions. An inmate's reputation or an officer's authority can be compromised at any time. Manipulation is one way to maintain control of daily interactions, by staying one step ahead of the other guy. Paluch envisions treatment approaches that might allow more authentic relations between prisoners and staff (and within each group as well), but none have been evident in his experience. (To review the literature on constructive coping in prison, see Johnson 2002.)

Sooner or later, deservedly or not, a long-term inmate is apt to find himself in the Restrictive Housing Unit, known as "the hole." This is maximum-security confinement, a prison within a prison. At one time in history punishment cells were buried underground and offered no amenities, hence the name "the hole." Prisoners lived on bread and water, without light, subject to abuses by staff.

Today's segregation cells are ordinary cells, in which inmates are fed regular, though often cold, meals. Nevertheless, the routine is an oppressive one. Upon entry, inmates are videotaped and strip-searched, then isolated in their cells for 24 hours a day. For one hour each day, prisoners are allowed outside, cuffed and shackled before being moved to kennel-sized recreation cages for limited exercise. Extreme as these conditions are, few prisoners rebel. Restrictive housing inmates want to do their time and return to the general population, where the food is a bit warmer and opportunities for socialization, recreation, and education are more available.

Prisons look more or less alike from the outside, seemingly interchangeable. Bales of concertina wire and towering cell blocks have dominated our perception of the world within. Paluch's experience, supported by research (Toch 1992), suggests that the appearance of uniformity is misleading. His experiences at SCI-Rockview and SCI-Frackville, for instance, are strikingly different.

At Frackville, Paluch ran into trouble with officials. When they were unresponsive to his many requests to correct freezing cell conditions, he wrote to an outside group for help. Guards saw him speaking with another inmate, who was about to cosign his letter, and demanded it be handed over. By official rules, a letter with more than one signature is a petition, which is prohibited. Paluch tore up the letter and refused to surrender the scraps. He was severely beaten and then written up on allegedly unfair charges. Paluch maintains that the letter was personal and posed no threat to prison security. However, the guards could not have known this, only that he was defying their authority. Violence by the staff was unnecessary and inexcusable in this situation, but one can see why they pushed the issue. Students may wish to ponder this unusual encounter to examine what went wrong and how all parties involved might have better managed the situation.

Each prison has its own history and culture. From Paluch's experiences, we learn that things are done quite differently at SCI-Rockview than at SCI-Frackville. Officers at Rockview carry out cell searches in a nonintrusive manner, treating prisoners' possessions with respect. At Frackville, by contrast, cells are trashed during searches, causing considerable resentment among inmates. One of Paluch's few serious run-ins with authority, as mentioned above, occurred at Frackville. This may reflect the heavy-handed way that Frackville's officers carried out their work or readers may assume that Paluch's negative experience colored his view of this institution, a possible subject for debate.

The important point is that prisons are not all the same, and each has a unique social climate that may be more or less suitable for a given individual. One approach to prison reform is to match people and environments, so that offenders are placed in settings that accommodate their individual adjustment strategies and reduce unnecessary friction (Toch 1992; Johnson 2002). To the credit of the Pennsylvania correctional system, Paluch was shipped out of Frackville, where he had trouble, and was allowed to start fresh at Rockview, where he experienced a better adjustment.

Institutions also change over time. Prison walls may be set in stone, but the culture within is more fluid and permeable. Prisons adapt to changes in the larger culture, just as prisoners do. They change in response to changing sentencing patterns, which alters the composition of the prison and the expectations of offenders who make up its population.

One salient change noted by Paluch is the emergence of a prison culture of snitches. Previously in prison history, snitching on fellow inmates was strictly forbidden, and "rats" were fair game for revenge. The situation today has changed. Prisoners serving longer sentences value the benefits—special favors—that come from cooperating with staff. It is one thing to snub one's nose at prison guards for a few years, quite another to do so for the rest of one's natural life. The result of inmates reporting problems to the staff and asking for their help, Paluch claims, is a safer prison environment.

Today, a misconduct report can have serious consequences for offenders. Predators are more inclined to back off if they know that their prospective victim will report them to the guards. Though I know of no existing research on this point, it is worth noting that Conover, a journalist turned correctional officer, observed that sexual violence was uncommon in New York State prisons, given that aggressors may be identified by victims and have to face added sanctions. Conover contended that prison rape was even less common than sex between male inmates and female staff (Conover 2001).

Lifers: Prison's Reluctant Citizens

Paluch is no fan of American prisons. But he has adapted well and sometimes finds positive features in his daily rounds, such as moments in the outdoors, feeding mess-hall crumbs to sparrows, or carrying out a daily list of domestic duties and obligations reminiscent of a soccer mom's. "It will be a busy day," he comments at one point. One cannot help but marvel at the human capacity to find activity and meaning under impossibly difficult circumstances.

Paluch writes with authority on prison life because he is a lifer. For better or worse, prison *is* his life. Lifers in Pennsylvania, all ineligible for parole, comprise some 4,000 inmates—10 percent of the prison population, including those sentenced at the tender age of 14. Paluch has spent many years behind bars. Like most lifers, he has matured and adapted himself admirably to his surroundings (Toch and Adams 2002; Johnson 2002). He is a member of an extended family united by sadness and regret, one of many who face the prospect of growing old and dying in prison.

"Lifers are my people," he states simply. For such men, prison is not a home of choice but the only home they have. As a result, they have come to value maturity and restraint. They do their time, mind their own business, avoid trouble, organize their days carefully, work hard, take advantage of programs, and try to make the most of the limited resources available to them in prison. In their view, other offenders with shorter sentences, in particular the young bucks, tend to be impetuous, selfish inmates who make noise without concern for their fellows; hassle the staff and make survival difficult for everyone; rob and steal, spreading fear; and litter, making the prison a dirty, uninviting place to live.

Lifers hope to one day find redemption in their lives and to help make prison a decent place to dwell in. As a result, they are a stabilizing force. A prison full of lifers is a much easier place in which to live and work than a prison full of short-sentenced inmates. Wardens have testified that lifers tend to be model prisoners (Johnson 2002). Nevertheless, model prisoners are not happy prisoners. Men like Paluch live day by day, minute by minute, trying to keep their thoughts *inside* the prison world rather than *outside* in the free world. They must cope with lost opportunities, the victims they have harmed, and the loved ones who miss them. Lifers carry within themselves a grim record of hopes and dreams gone sour.

Recounting case examples, Paluch relates the story of young Joshua, a lifer from a good family who succumbs to drugs and takes his own life. His tragic demise is handled by the prison staff with bureaucratic indifference. Another is the story of Mr. Dead Man Walking, an aging lifer who worked outside prison walls for many years in a prison forestry program but, due to changes in the political climate, was reincarcerated despite model behavior and repeated appeals for clemency. These stories and others like them form a bitter residue in the minds of lifers like Paluch, who himself struggles to maintain hope against difficult odds.

A source of deep pain for lifers is the fact that their loved ones suffer with them and because of them. For relatives as well as inmates, the crime and the punishment are an ongoing nightmare that all must live with indefinitely, each and every day of their lives. Students will read personal testimonies from Paluch's devoted father, from the mother of two sons doing life, and from a woman who married a lifer in prison and has stuck by him for 20 years. The support of loved ones is a lifeline deeply appreciated by lifers, their shared adversity sometimes bringing family members closer together, as in Paluch's own story.

Life sentences, however, do not typically heal breaches in families nor spawn stable relationships, let alone lasting marriages. More often than not, loved ones grow weary of calling or visiting lifers and frequently give up on them. Wives find new husbands, children grow up and away from their imprisoned fathers, and parents age and die. For many lifers, the day may come when there is no one left outside to write or visit. At this tragic juncture, lifers think of themselves as a kind of living dead, condemned beings whose bodies are physically alive but whose souls are dead or dying.

James A. Paluch, Jr., lives every day with his crime and the terrible harm that it has caused. He hopes that this book will in some way redeem him by contributing to society's understanding of prison life. In my opinion, he has certainly done his part. Readers are invited to join Paluch in his grim but compelling prison world, to learn new insights about these institutions, and to ponder whether justice is served by sentences that amount to a slow death by indifference and neglect.

Sources

Conover, Ted. (2001). *Newjack: Guarding Sing-Sing*. New York, NY: Knopf.

Johnson, Robert. (2002). *Hard Time: Understanding and Reforming the Prison*, 3rd ed. Belmont, CA: Wadsworth.

Lombardo, Lucien. (1989). *Guards Imprisoned: Correctional Officers at Work*, 2nd ed. Cincinnati, OH: Anderson.

Sykes, Gresham. (1956/1971). *The Society of Captives: A Study of a Maximum-Security Prison*. Princeton, NJ: Princeton University Press.

Toch, Hans. (1992). *Living in Prison: The Ecology of Survival*, revised ed. Washington, DC: American Psychological Association.

Toch, Hans, and Kenneth Adams. (2002). *Acting Out: Maladaptation Behavior in Confinement*. Washington, DC: American Psychological Association. ✦

Part I

Life in Prison

Chapter 1

As I Write This Book . . .

Sometimes, I get so tired of looking at this typewriter that I do my best to avoid using it. But other times, this machine seems to be the only thing in the world that is always there for me. I take care of it, clean it, give it proper maintenance, and cover it to keep out the dust. In return, it is always there for me when I need it.

I am sitting at my desk now, giving my fingers a well-deserved break. Outside my cell, I hear two prisoners arguing over last night's boxing match. In a respectful tone, I ask these strangers to keep the noise down and take their debate somewhere else. "My fault, o'head," one of them apologizes, and they walk away.

I ask myself, did this guy just call me "o'head?" Meaning "old head," this is a common prison phrase that refers to an older, well-respected inmate. Another term, "young buck," is used to address or describe a younger person. I would have preferred to have been called "young buck." After all, I am only 29 years old.

I turn around and stand over my toilet to relieve myself, keeping my back to the cell door for privacy purposes. I wipe the rim of the toilet and flush it, then push two metal buttons on my sink to produce a spurt of water, so I can wash my hands. Then I wipe my hands on a towel that hangs from the front of my bed.

I sit back in my desk chair and pick up the Snickers bar on my desk. I earned it yesterday from an inmate for typing a one-page letter to his lawyer. Snickers bars are my favorite. At lunch today, I did not eat the nasty tuna-noodle casserole that was served, and I could almost hear this sweet snack beckoning me to come back to my cell and slowly eat it.

On the outside of the candy wrapper is an advertisement that reads, *CLASSIC OR CLUNKER?* Underneath, it says, *You could win*

3

one of a hundred cars—some absolute classics and some real clunkers. Look inside to see. At the moment I am more interested in satisfying my sweet tooth than in finding out whether I won a car.

I look inside the wrapper and read, *Sorry, this is not an instant winner.* It also tells me that first prize is a 1957 Ford Thunderbird convertible. I savor the taste of the candy bar and wonder what the world would think if I had indeed won the prize. Would I be able to claim it? After all, I purchased the Snickers from the prison commissary. Perhaps my family could claim it. Or I could find a car collector willing to purchase it from me for, say, $75,000. Then I could use the money to hire a famous lawyer like F. Lee Bailey to handle my case. But since the Pennsylvania Supreme Court recently denied my appeal anyway, I forget the whole thing and take another bite of the candy bar.

Chewing slowly, I look around my cell. Its walls and floor are constructed of dense, pockmarked concrete, except for the thick iron bars that enclose the cell front and its door. My present cell measures 10 feet long, seven feet wide, and nine feet high. To most of us, these cells are nothing more than cold coffins, leaving a chilling effect on anyone forced to live inside them.

On one wall hangs a calendar that reminds me of all the days gone by and the many days yet to come. Under the calendar, on top of a cabinet, sits my television set. I do not pay for cable.[1] I am thrifty and would rather spend the money on stationery and other supplies. Besides, television can consume a prisoner's time and distract him from focusing on his real priorities: legal work, school, etc.

Next to the television set is another cabinet that holds my bookshelf and my typewriter. I have my own library of religious materials, legal self-help guides, and educational materials, along with some composition books that contain personal poetry and other writings.

Near my poetry books stands a Polaroid picture of my father, my baby sister, and myself when they visited me in prison last year. It serves as a constant reminder to keep a positive attitude and do what is right. Beside that is another photo of my father holding my sister's baby. When I met my nephew for the first time, my heart melted. It became one more reason to keep hoping.

Above those pictures on the wall is my anti-death penalty poster, which shows a hand holding a stone. The poster reads, *Jesus was once asked for his support of the death penalty. His reply: "Let the one who is without sin cast the first stone."*

Next to the poster is a Star of David flag that I made myself, a reminder to never forget the homeland of my ancestors, a place I hope to see one day and perhaps to die in. Beside this is the Hebrew word *Israyl*, which is also my creation. Next to this is a cartoon of Patrick Roy, my favorite NHL goalie, and some clippings from newspapers that published letters that I wrote on "lifer" issues. Below this is a photograph of the U.S. Women's Soccer Team.

The final item on my wall is a poster that shows a frog in a stork's mouth. The frog has his hands around the stork's neck. Its caption reads, *Never give up!* This is my motto.

I look again at the Polaroid picture of me standing between my father and my baby sister. It is time to go back to work.

Endnote

1. Television cable is available to prisoners in the Pennsylvania Department of Corrections (PA DOC) who are able to pay for this service. At the present time, the PA DOC has a contract with Correctional Cable, which charges prisoners $18.50 per month for cable service. ✦

Chapter 2

Bof's[1] Journal

James Anthony Paluch, Jr.
Born: May 24, 1971.
Height: 6'3"
Weight: 195 lbs.
Brown hair, green eyes, wears glasses.
Hometown: Allentown, PA.
Ethnic heritage: Polish/Slovak-American.
Religion: Messianic Yahwist.

Enjoys football, soccer, bowling, poetry, prose, studies on psychology, sociology, political science, and history.

Arrested June 8, 1990, in Philadelphia, PA, for first-degree murder and aggravated assault.

Sentenced October, 1991, to life imprisonment for murder (a sentence which in Pennsylvania currently carries no possibility of parole), along with five to 10 years for aggravated assault, to be served concurrently.

Philadelphia Detention Center: June, 1990–June, 1991.

I want to die. I am not supposed to be here. This place is for bad people. What happened? I am very confused and very scared. I am afraid I may be assaulted or even killed. I just celebrated my 19th birthday two weeks ago. Where is my family? Where is my girlfriend? When am I going to get out of here? I want to die. . . .

The guards come to my cell to tell me that my life is in danger. They put me in the Mental Health Unit until they can figure out what to do with me. . . .

I call home to tell my family I am okay. My mother was recently diagnosed with ovarian cancer and is very sick. She encourages me to read the Bible. . . .

I go to court today for some type of hearing. On the bus trip back, another prisoner attacks me. . . .

I speak to the doctor today on the Mental Health Unit. I cannot live like this. I find myself alone and crying. Men are not supposed to cry. I feel defeated and unworthy to continue living. The doctor puts me on some type of antidepressant medication, but I do not have a clue what it is. . . .

The cells are very cold. The air conditioner is on at all hours in order to make us sleep more, so we are less of a problem for the staff. . . .

Sometimes, they let us out of our cells to watch television. Everybody likes to watch Sanford and Son, *but this is the first time I have ever seen it. . . .*

I find a roach in my cell this morning and go crazy trying to kill it. I hate those damn things. . . .

They take my Dilantin[2] and other medications, mix them with water, and force me to drink the mixture. It burns my mouth and throat. . . .

To occupy my time, I write letters, draw, and read books that my mother gives me on her monthly visits with my father. My girlfriend has stopped writing me, even though I write her three or four times a week. . . .

They place me back in general population. My meals are delivered to my cell, so I do not eat in the dining hall with the other inmates. Every day, I am escorted to the medication line. . . .

I buy a small Walkman from the commissary, so I can listen to music all day long. I am still very depressed. . . .

The food is terrible. They serve these round, hard pieces of meatloaf that the prisoners call "hockey pucks." The chicken legs are so huge that they are known as "pterodactyl legs.". . .

There are so many roaches and mice in this place that I spend nearly half the time in my cell trying to chase them out. This is a disgusting and filthy place. . . .

This evening, a prisoner accused of murder hangs himself in his cell. I say a prayer for his family. . . .

There is a fight today on the block. Through my cell door, I observe two prisoners severely beating down a third, while two more inmates watch. The guards wait until the fight is over. . . .

As I return from the library, a prisoner spits in my face. I have no idea who he is. . . .

My mother visits one last time before Christmas, too weak to make another trip. I later learn from my father that she cried all the way home. Before she leaves, she gives me a Hershey's Kiss with an almond in it, which she smuggled in. . . .

I call my girlfriend. She tells me she lost our baby, who was a boy. She made a statement to the police at the time of my arrest, but she assures me that she will never testify against me. . . .

I call my court-appointed lawyer's office, but he is never there. His secretary tells me that the district attorney is seeking the death penalty against me. I want to die, but I am too much of a coward to take my own life. I do not tell my parents about this. . . .

I phone home and spend nearly 20 minutes talking to my mother. I tell her how much I love her, and she tells me the same. I sense that this will be the last time I will ever speak to her. . . .

When I first arrive at the Detention Center, I am over 200 pounds. Nine months later, the nurse tells me I weigh 130 pounds. . . .

On the phone, my father regrets that he has bad news. "I know," I reply. He says my court-appointed lawyer will notify the prison in order to make arrangements for me to attend my mother's funeral. . . .

I do not hear anything, so I call my lawyer's office again. The secretary apologizes for not contacting the prison. They procure a court order to have the sheriff's department escort me to the funeral home, but the sheriff refuses to honor it, because they require 48-hours notice. . . .

The prisoner housed next door to me just came back from court. Less than three hours ago, a jury sentenced him to death.

Holmesburg Prison: June, 1991–August, 1991.

I am transferred to a maximum-security prison that prisoners call "The Terrordome." My cell is infested with all kinds of roaches. I complain to the guards, and they give me four glue traps for trapping mice. I put them in the four corners of my cell. In the morning, they are all filled with roaches. . . .

The gigantic roaches in here are called "water bugs." Prisoners put them in milk cartons, so they can fight against each other. They bet on which roach will win. . . .

I am taking a shower, when I turn to see a big, fat rat facing me. Instead of running away, he seems to be staring me down. I throw my shampoo bottle at him, but he just calmly waddles away toward a hole in the wall. . . .

I witness a prisoner getting stabbed today near the end of the block. The guards lock themselves in on the other side of the gate.

Philadelphia Industrial Correctional Center: August, 1991–October, 1991.

I am transferred to PICC as I prepare to go to trial. This is a fairly new prison that is much cleaner than the Detention Center or Holmesburg, but the food is terrible. . . .

I meet a prisoner here in his 70s, a former attorney for a bank. He knows my court-appointed lawyer and warns me that I will not receive effective counsel. He advises me on my case. . . .

I call my girlfriend, but she hangs up on me. . . .

I go to court for a hearing. The DA says that my girlfriend will testify against me at trial. My court-appointed lawyer says that his strategy is to blame her for the shootings. I will never agree to this, and I am sure that she will not testify against me. . . .

The DA offers a deal: if I plead guilty to first-degree murder, I will be sentenced to life imprisonment instead of death. But my ex-lawyer inmate friend advises me not to do it. I tell the DA that I will only plead guilty to third-degree murder, which carries a maximum 20-year sentence.[3] The DA laughs in my face. . . .

My trial begins, and my ex-girlfriend testifies against me. Some of her testimony is true, but some of it is a lie. I believe that she has been coerced into lying by the homicide detectives. I can see that she is scared, but I still feel betrayed and sick to my stomach. . . .

I want to take the stand and tell the jury exactly what happened. But my lawyer warns that I may provoke the jury into giving me the death penalty. I tell the judge that I want to take the stand, but that I will not be doing so on the advice of my attorney . . .

The trial lasts six days. I am found guilty of first-degree murder.

Courtroom 285, City Hall: October 4, 1991.

"In the case of the Commonwealth of Pennsylvania v. James Paluch, *on Bill Number 2445, June Term, 1990, in which you found the defendant guilty of first-degree murder, have you found any aggravating circumstances?"*

"No."

"Have you found any mitigating circumstances?"

"The mitigating circumstances outweigh the aggravating circumstances."

"What is your sentence?"

"Life."

When the sentence is pronounced, I lose control of my bodily functions and urinate on myself.

State Correctional Institution at Graterford: October, 1991– March, 1992.

The bus enters the driveway at SCI-Graterford,[5] and I see the huge wall that surrounds the prison. I am scared to death. I have heard many things about this place, all of them evil. I am a tall, thin "boy" with no "fight game" to protect myself. If I get raped, I will definitely kill myself. Hell, I am probably going to die here anyway. There is no way someone like me is going to make it in here. . . .

I am given a new identity, "BQ-3769," and placed on AC status[6] for my own protection while I am being classified to another prison. . . .

My first cellmate is a young "boy" just like myself. He offers to perform oral sex on me. I request another cellmate. . . .

My second cellmate is an enormously obese man who is on AC status because he ran up drug bills with other prisoners to feed his addiction. I find him personally disgusting. I request another cellmate. . . .

My new cellmate seems to have mental problems. He talks all the time about how he is going to kill his brother when he gets out. He has a television set but will not let me watch it. He takes my commissary items. If I try to fight him, I am sure he will get the best of me. I ask to be moved to another cell, but the lieutenant refuses. "This is not a hotel," he says. . . .

My cellmate threatens to assault me if I do not move out of the cell. I send request slips to the captain, as well as the superintendent, requesting to be moved. No one answers my pleas. . . .

My cellmate gives me three days to move out, or he will beat my brains out. I am scared to death of this moron. I think about attacking him first, but I do not want to pay the consequences. The guy in the next cell gives me the address of the Governor's office and suggests that I address my com-

plaint there. I do not know what else to do, so I send a letter to the Governor. . . .

My cellmate now says that I have until the end of the day to get out of the cell. I speak to every staff member who comes by, but they all say I cannot be moved. As a last resort, I fake a suicide attempt—if you can believe this—by allowing my cellmate to make bruises around my neck with a sheet. When the lieutenant sees the bruises, he moves me to the Mental Health Unit (MHU). . . .

The MHU is air conditioned, despite the fact that it is winter. The nurses have me on suicide watch, but I have no intention of taking my own life. I reluctantly take Sinequon and another anti-depressant.[7] Other prisoners here appear to have many mental disorders, but none seem like a threat to me. In fact, I make a few acquaintances. . . .

I am taken to the Security Office. My letter to the Governor, they inform me, has been sent back to SCI-Graterford. I explain what happened, and they ask why I did not request a move. I tell them that I did. . . .

Another MHU prisoner and I get into an argument. He pushes me and I push him back. I am given my first "misconduct report" for fighting. I serve 30 days "disciplinary custody"[8] in the MHU, then am released back onto AC status in the Restrictive Housing Unit. . . .

I make a phone call home to my father. Before I hang up, he tells me he loves me. It has been a long time since I have heard these words. . . .

My counselor stops by today and tells me that I have been classified to SCI-Huntingdon. As he walks away, he says, "Good luck."

*   *   *

There's a Hole . . .

There's a hole in my wall
(chip, chip) . . .
(scrape, scrape) . . .
Okay, I made it outside.

There's a hole in the ground
(dig, dig) . . .
(clump, clump) . . .
Okay, I have my freedom.

I run down a hill
(swoosh, swoosh) . . .
(hurry, hurry) . . .
Okay, I made it to the river.

I swim across the river
(splash, splash) . . .
(breathe, breathe) . . .
Okay, I made it to the highway.

I hear the prison siren
(wwhwwhwwhwwhwwh) . . .
(whistle, whistle) . . .
I run like hell.

I hear the dogs
(bark, bark) . . .
(whimper, whimper) . . .
I still run like hell.

There's a telephone
(ring, ring) . . .
(hello, hello) . . .
Please come get me.

There's a car coming towards me
(click, click) . . .
(shut, shut) . . .
We drive away.

I hear a sound
(clank, clank) . . .
(open, open) . . .
Breakfast is here and I wake up!

Endnotes

1. The author's nickname is "Bof." The statements in this chapter were recorded in composition books I call "Bof's Journal," and were selected by the editor, Thomas J. Bernard.
2. Dilantin is an anti-epileptic prescription medication.
3. In 1995, the Pennsylvania General Assembly changed the sanction for third-degree murder from 10–20 years to 20–40 years.
4. A life-sentence is also commonly referred to as a "wheel," a punishment in perpetual motion that continues until the prisoner's life expires; hence in Pennsylvania, a virtual death sentence.
5. "State Correctional Institution" is normally abbreviated SCI.
6. Administrative custody (AC), means that an inmate is placed in "Restrictive housing" for his own protection, rather than as a punishment for an infraction (disciplinary custody).
7. When the author was transferred to SCI-Huntingdon in March, 1992, he refused to take psychotropic medications in the belief that had he continued to ingest "mind-altering poisons" his normal cognitive functions would have digressed and been adverse to the goal of rehabilitation. See Chapter 18.
8. Disciplinary custody means that the inmate is placed in "Restrictive housing" because of an infraction. In this case, he served this in his own cell in the Mental Health Unit (MHU), rather than being moved to the Restrictive Housing Unit (RHU). See above, endnote 6. ✦

Chapter 3

Enter the Madness

In all 26 State Correctional Institutions across Pennsylvania, bells, sirens, and buzzers sound throughout the day. They start at 6 A.M. for standing counts, then at 7:30 A.M. for breakfast lines. Then comes dinner (actually lunch) and supper, then more standing counts. Prisoners hear these bells, sirens, and buzzers a minimum of 10 times a day, 70 times a week, 3,640 times a year.

Sometimes, I wish I could rip out all the wires carrying the electric current that causes these annoying sounds. It is not that I have any criminal intentions of destroying state property, but for a very long time I have yearned for just one single day of peace.

If you have never been inside a prison, it is hard to imagine the *noise.* Place yourself inside a room where everything around you is concrete and steel. When you speak, your voice echoes off the walls, amplifying everything you say. Now imagine 50 people doing the same thing: you cannot quite hear what someone else is saying to you, so you naturally speak a little louder. Soon, everyone is talking so loud that a silent person hears nothing but a constant rumble. The insanity manifests itself in the strains and echoes of voices full of anger, fear, ignorance, and frustration.

When you first come to prison, it is very hard to adjust to the noise level. In the beginning, it is nearly impossible to sleep or rest. Normal sleep is interrupted interminably. If you have a headache, it becomes worse. Eventually, your body becomes too tired to fight, so you sleep despite the loud clamor. Some prisoners take prescription medications to make them drowsy, so the adjustment is easier, but these medications make it harder to function normally when they are awake.

On the average, inmates sleep between 10 P.M. and 8 A.M. During these hours, they try to keep any noise confined to their cells. The noise level usually subsides unless, for example, there is a late sports event on television that provokes loud excitement, such as clapping, screaming, or whistling. Some prisoners stay up until two or three in the morning, then sleep through breakfast.

All prisoners are required to awake at 6:00 A.M. for a standing count, which can take from 10 minutes to half an hour. Then they can go back to bed until breakfast lines are called. This is when the normal noise level of the day begins.

Until evening lock-up, the noise is now so constant that you are forced to tolerate it. Eventually, you become desensitized to it. You know it exists, but it becomes so routine that it seems normal. Yet psychologically, it is harmful to desensitize yourself to what in the normal world would be tantamount to clinical insanity.

It is difficult for staff members to deal with the noise as well, but after eight hours, they return to a comparatively quieter outside world. Yet they still have to deal with both worlds, and according to some guards I have spoken to it does become an underlying pressure for them.

It is not just the loud, drowning voices of the ignorant and the sorrowful, but the bells, sirens, and fire alarms, and the earsplitting microphones that are often so strident that you cannot understand what is being said or even hear yourself think.

In the evenings, when the television sets are on and prisoners congregate during "block-out,"[1] the noise reaches its peak. Even those who decide to stay in their own cells must turn up the volume of their sets to drown out the constant racket.

Some prisoners often turn up their radios to a particular song they like. If it is a rap song, the white inmates might become aggravated and object. If it is heavy metal, black inmates might shout, "Turn that devil music down!"

From day to day, the noise continues. You may wonder how any man can tolerate its madness. If your nerves are weak, the madness will get to you. You will eventually lose touch with any sanity that you have managed to cling to. Once that grip on reality is lost, so are you.

Most of us either ignore the noise or inure ourselves to it. Either way, it continues to exist as a never-ending presence in the lives of prisoners. To express my own frustration over this endless din would only contribute to the madness, so I do my best to simply shut it out of my mind.

*   *   *

They are at it again tonight, screaming and hollering senselessly. "Turn the f**king heat on! Muthaf**kers, turn the goddamn heat on!!" The complaints usually start with a single individual, then soon others join in, until all you can hear are echoes drowning each other out.

It is winter, and for many prisoners on this housing unit it is unbearably cold. You can put on thermal long-johns and extra clothes, cover yourself in blankets, and still feel half frozen.

As I reach for my TV headphones to protect my ears from the unpleasant disturbance, more voices join in: "Keep the f**kin' heat *off!* We don't want no heat!! F**k the heat!" The noise worsens, and I feel sympathy for any inmate trying to sleep.

Here at SCI-Rockview,[2] there are two main housing units, each of which is five tiers high. The voices that demand more heat come from the bottom tiers. Those who want the heat shut off resound from the top tiers.

The problem is that heat rises. On the highest tiers when the heat is on, it is too hot to even breathe, resulting in irritable and frustrated inmates. But those on the lower tiers experience refrigerator-like temperatures that are also very uncomfortable. Thus is the reality of prison living conditions in these housing units.

There are no ceiling fans to circulate the air or push it downward. A few years ago, Rockview was court-ordered to install two ventilation shafts on each side of the housing units. A system was installed, but all it really does is collect dust and blow it back out, making our cells dustier and dirtier than before. Many prisoners, such as asthmatics, experience respiratory problems as a result.

In reaction to the imbalance of heat, prisoners begin arguing with each other. Someone on the bottom tier yells to another upstairs to take his clothes off if it is too hot. In response, the upstairs prisoner yells back, "If you're cold, f**k your damn celly (cellmate)!" A few prisoners can be heard chuckling over this remark.

The entire disturbance lasts about five minutes. Sometimes, it will cease only to start up again later. Inmates have been complaining about the heating problem year after year after year. Our keepers tell us that they will get around to correcting it. But their promises, like the senseless noises I am forced to endure at this very moment, go unheeded.

I turn off my television set. It is late. I think about my family, who are probably sleeping in peaceful silence in a warm, comfortable bed. I close my eyes, but I cannot sleep.

Endnotes

1. "Block-out" is the period when inmates are in the cell block but can roam outside their cells. During this time, many of them congregate in common areas, where there are usually tables and chairs. They may play games, especially card games and board games, watch television, or just socialize.
2. Every prison in Pennsylvania is called a "State Correctional Institution," abbreviated as SCI. Thus, this is the State Correctional Institution at Rockview. ✦

Part II

Food

Chapter 4

The Old Dining Hall

After the 6 A.M. standing count, I usually go back to bed or meditate on what I am going to do today, which is usually the same thing every day. Most mornings, I read *The Book of Yahweh* (the Holy Scriptures). This particular morning, I am exhausted, so I go back to sleep. Since the staff daily rotates the order of housing units that report to the meal lines, I know that this morning we will be eating last, which is good reason to go back to bed.

An hour later, our bell rings for breakfast lines. I don my eyeglasses and hurry to put on my "browns" (i.e., my prisoner clothes, which are a kind of cocoa brown), my boots, and my winter coat. I reach inside my medicine cabinet for a vitamin bottle and take out a breakfast pill. For me, vitamins are a daily investment in keeping healthy.

Outside my cell, I hear countless doors click open and clank shut, followed by the sound of combination locks snapping closed. Within two minutes, I am ready to go. I grab my own lock, open my cell door, close it, and set the lock on the door to discourage thieves from stealing my personal belongings while I am gone.

I head down the range, sometimes trying to pass the slower flow of moving bodies. Cell doors are still opening, so I must be careful. Many inmates do not look before they exit, so their doors often swing open wildly in front of me. I reach the steel staircase at the end of the tier and descend to the main floor. Then I exit the main entrance of the housing unit and wend through the crowded traffic outside to meet a friend as I usually do each morning.

Just outside the main entrance it is nearly total daylight, and the birds are waiting for me. My babies are chirping on the razor wire overhead, greeting me. I reach inside my coat pocket for pieces of bread hidden from last night's supper. As I always do, I make a clicking sound with my tongue that they recognize. They fly nearby without getting too close. Unlike the parakeets I grew up with, these birds are wild and safety-conscious. I crumble the bread then throw it to them. Sparrows, European Starlings, and rock doves (pigeons) flutter closer to retrieve the bread, then fly away back to their nests. I hurry along to reach my friend.

In some prisons, inmates cross from the housing units to the dining hall without going outside. But here at Rockview, we must walk outside to a separate building. Inmates often complain about this, especially when it rains. For me, however, the opportunity to breathe fresh air is worth the trip. It allows me a chance to see the beautiful trees and flowers on the prison grounds (at least during the warmer seasons) and the flocking of colorful birds. The walk to the dining hall is a time to look forward to, as I am no longer confined to my 10-foot-by-seven-foot cell.

This is also the time to say hello to friends. The one I am expecting says, "Good morning," and I return the salutation. I am hungry, and by the way my colleague is hurrying, I suspect that he is, too.

* * *

At the moment, the dining hall is under construction, the huge room divided in half. One half is closed off, so we use the second half. When the first half is completed, we will switch to that side while the other half is under construction. This side will be remodeled into two separate dining halls, thereby creating three smaller rooms instead of one large, single one.

This morning, the serving line is a little longer. The "menu," if it can be called that, is coffee cake, grits, yogurt, toast, oleo, milk, coffee, and sugar. As I approach the food line, a large aluminum tray rack sits on wheels to my left. I pull out a plastic tray and inspect it for cleanliness. No, not this one—it has gravy on it from last night's supper. I pick another one. Not this one either—there are dirt particles on it. I try a different section of the rack, but to my annoyance, the next tray is just as dirty. Will I ever get lucky and find myself a clean tray?

After picking out seven or eight trays, to the mutual annoyance of inmates behind me, I finally find one that appears to be clean. Cleanliness is important to me, especially considering that hepatitis plagues our prison system.[1] But to my fellow prisoners, I am just another complainer looking for an issue to play with. They do not quite understand the importance of a clean tray, nor do they really care about their health.

Next stop, plastic cups. The same dilemma. I pick up a few cups that have dirt or food particles stuck to the sides. After setting aside six or seven dirty cups, I find what appears to be a clean one.

Like a treasure hunt, I have found the first two items. Now the challenge is to locate the final item: a clean set of utensils wrapped in a white napkin. Many of them have pieces of rice lodged between the prongs of the fork, the knives and spoons often soiled as well. The inmate assigned to dispensing eating utensils hands me a set. I inspect the utensils very carefully. Ahh . . . my first selection appears to be clean. I am now ready for the last stretch of the journey.

As the line slowly moves on, I slide my tray along the aluminum serving line. Plastic sneeze guards allow me to view the so-called menu. A rectangle metal pan of oleo (not butter) is served first. The oleo dispenser seems less than enthusiastic about having to stand there for an hour and a half, let alone looking at thousands of men who wish it were real butter. As usual, I do him a favor and skip the oleo.

Next to him, an inmate serves what appears to be yogurt, a generic brand that tastes like liquidy sour cream. It is nasty, so I pass on the "yogurt." So far, my score is 0 for 2 on the meal.

Next is an inmate serving grits. Cream of wheat, yes, but grits, no. I do not particularly care for grits and only eat them if I am extremely hungry. Besides, there are often large, lumpy balls of uncooked grits mixed in. I pass. Like a team wondering if it is ever going to make the playoffs, I am now 0 for 3.

The next dispenser is serving coffee cake and toast. These look digestible to me, and he places the items on my tray. Then I hand my plastic coffee cup to the final server, who dumps two tablespoons of sugar into it.

As I turn to the metal tables serving milk and coffee, I notice the Food Services Instructor (FSI) closely watching the inmate kitchen workers. Like a watchdog, the FSI will growl and snarl when a dispenser serves more than the amount of food a prisoner is supposed to receive. However, there are times when an FSI will permit kitchen servers to give a little extra, for which many inmates are very grateful.

I approach the milk-serving table, on which there are many filled plastic cups. Since the milk is already poured, I cannot inspect the cups for cleanliness. I do not like this, but I choose one anyway.

I move on to the table with a large aluminum coffee pot. Inmates tell me that it is not really coffee, but chicory. Whatever it is, it does not taste like coffee at all. I pour some of the sugar out of my coffee cup and fill the cup halfway with "coffee." The pot has a nozzle that I and about 500 other inmates have touched in order to fill our cups. I always worry about hepatitis, and this seems unsanitary to me. There are other ways to dispense coffee without subjecting us to this risk. I have sent two request slips to the Culinary manager about this, but no one has responded to my complaints nor taken any measures to correct the problem. As far as I know, they simply do not care.

My friend heads for the tables and I follow close behind. We usually try to sit together at the same table, but it does not always work out that way. This morning, we are the lucky first two at an open table that seats a maximum of four. Prisoners cannot sit at any table they want to, always directed by a guard to the next vacant row of seats as inmates emerge from the food lines.

I look at the table to see if it is clean. It appears to be, though things are not always as they appear. I set down my tray and re-move my brown coat. I check the seat to make sure it is clean too, then sit down with the coat on my lap.

Before I begin my meal, I bow my head for silent prayer: "Thank you, Yahweh, for the meal you have provided me. May it give me the strength and fortitude to do Your will this day. Allelu Yahweh." It is only a simple blessing, and each day my prayers vary some-what.

Though I do not particularly enjoy this kind of breakfast, I ac-cept what I do have out of a sense of tolerance. The coffee cake is fairly small this morning. Some mornings, I am fortunate to have a bigger piece, but not today. It is also hard and not moist. It is called coffee cake, but there are no crumbs on top of it. It is little more than a baked mixture of flour, eggs, and sugar. Four bites, and it is gone.

I do not normally eat the toast unless the meal line also serves jelly, even though the toast here is pretty good. At my last prison, the bread was processed through a big "toaster" machine that did not actually toast the bread but instead made it stale.

This morning, I wrap my two small pieces of toast in a paper napkin and slip them inside my pocket. Some would call it stealing, but I do not. The food on my tray was given to me, so I consider it mine. Though Department of Corrections rules prohibit taking food out of the dining hall, I choose to disregard these rules. Inmates take food out for many different reasons. They may want to eat a portion later or perhaps have made a deal to give it to someone else. I take it for my babies . . . my bird friends.

As I sip my milk, I ponder what I am going to do for the rest of the day. When I get back to the housing unit, a friend will have some newspapers for me to read. My cell needs to be swept out, and I have some dirty laundry that needs to be washed. My plastic wash-tub is cracked, so I may have to borrow one from my neighbor. I have paperwork to write for the Pennsylvania Lifers' Association at Rockview (PLAR), an inmate organization of which I am an officer, then I have to type it up. This reminds me that I want to ask the staff liaison to the PLAR about possibly purchasing a new typewriter. Lastly, I have a Lifers' board meeting tonight, which I have to prepare for. This will be a busy day.

I take another sip of milk, then look around me for any other friends sitting nearby. I see Mr. Plum, and in a few seconds our eyes meet. He smiles, and I nod my head in acknowledgment.

When we have a good breakfast, such as pancakes or scrambled eggs, the dining hall is usually crowded. This morning, attendance is moderate. The two strangers sitting at my table are having a private conversation. Although I can hear what they are talking about, it is none of my business, so I tune it out. My companion is quiet this morning. Perhaps, he too is pondering how to get through the day, but who knows? I wash down the vitamin pill in my pocket with the remaining milk. A lieutenant (we call them "white hats") walks by and stands next to the wall, observing all the action in the dining hall.

My friend finishes his meal and lets me know that he is ready to leave. I gulp down the last of my coffee, excuse myself, and rise. I put on my brown coat, pick up my tray, and head for the exit door. I dump the leftovers on my tray into a garbage container, drop my plastic utensils into one dishwashing tray and the cup and bowls into another, then place my tray on a stack of dirty trays.

The guard at the door inspects me as I leave, his job to make sure each and every inmate gives back each and every plastic serving utensil. Then I am out of the dining hall, down the hallway, and out of the building.

Endnote

1. The Centers for Disease Control, an agency of the federal government, has found as many as 43 percent of inmates in particular prisons infected with hepatitis. About 25 percent of Pennsylvania inmates test positive for the disease, which attacks and ultimately destroys the liver. Beginning in 2002, the Pennsylvania Department of Corrections has undertaken an education and voluntary immunization program for both staff and inmates. See Jennifer Lin and Mark Fazlollah, "Prisoner Unlocks Hepatitis C Epidemic," *Philadelphia Inquirer*, July 22, 2002. ✦

Chapter 5

The New Dining Hall

The dining hall at SCI-Rockview used to be one large gathering place. But due to security concerns—prison officials' fear of riots or mass disturbances—the new construction has now split the dining hall into three separate dining areas. Cameras have also been installed in each of the new halls, I would assume to monitor such threats. Like the endless miles of razor wire that surround this prison, these new measures are again reminders of my incarceration.

Before the construction, prisoners could choose what kinds of food they wanted on their trays. For instance, if a prisoner did not want spinach, he could just pass by the inmate worker serving spinach. After the construction, however, prisoners now stand in line and move towards a small window, through which food trays are handed to them. Each food tray is basically prepared the same way.

Also in the past, each institution served its own menu. Now, however, the Pennsylvania Department of Corrections mandates that each institution must abide by a master menu list. Basically, the same meals are served in prisons across the state. Some institutions serve better quality of foods than others, but the quantity of food remains barely sufficient to satisfy anyone's appetite.

Prisoners who do not eat meat or do not like the main course may request the "alternative protein" menu. Each dinner and supper includes an alternative protein, such as garbanzo beans, soy burgers, tofu, peanut butter, bean paste, or cottage cheese. However, these alternative proteins are often less desirable than the regular meals.

* * *

As I stand in line in one of the new dining halls for supper, I can see inmate food servers through large Plexiglas windows. Each tray passes from one worker to the next as if on an assembly line. I gesture to one of the servers to give me a little more mashed potatoes. He simply shrugs his shoulders helplessly, since an FSI monitors his every move. I am handed my food tray and a cup of grape drink, then a guard directs me to a table as usual.

As part of the new construction, the old tables have been replaced with new metal ones, some of which seat three prisoners, others seating four. Before I sit down, I notice that the table is not clean. I motion to an inmate kitchen worker known as a "table wiper" to come and clean the table.

His cleaning rag is so dirty that I and three other waiting prisoners complain and request that he replace it with a clean one. "I already told my supervisor," says the table wiper. "He said there is nothing he can do."

I look around for a "white hat" to complain to, but there are none. Only two guards are in this dining hall, which seats approximately 120 prisoners at a time, and I know that my complaints will fall on deaf ears. So I sit, bow my head, say a short prayer, and begin to eat.

The posted menu at the housing unit advertised "Veal Italiano," but there is nothing Italian about this veal. It looks and tastes like a breaded hamburger. Yesterday, they served "Polish Kielbasa," but in reality it was nothing more than a piece of processed sausage. I grew up on Polish food, and calling this kielbasa is an insult to my ancestors.

Served with the veal is a portion of red sauce with large amounts of pepper in it. If I wanted pepper in my sauce, I could have used the pepper shaker on the table. The pasta shells are overcooked and sticking to one another. The cole slaw is basically shredded cabbage soaked in vinegar—totally unappetizing. Rockview used to serve four slices of bread at dinner and supper, but now we receive only two slices. This evening, the bread is hard and stale.

The best thing served on the tray is a small piece of peach cake with a thin coating of white icing. I am tempted to trade my veal for someone else's cake. Instead, I tolerate eating the meat simply because I am hungry. For a brief moment, I harbor a craving for a juicy McDonald's Big Mac with large fries. I also remember how good the meals were that my mother cooked, and I long desperately for their savory taste.

As I sip my grape drink, I notice that the inside of the cup is dirty. Before the construction, prisoners could check their food tray, utensils, cups, etc., to make sure they were clean before the food was placed in them. We can no longer do this, now subjected to potentially unclean and unsanitary dining conditions. Inmates have no way to know now if their food is contaminated, though of course most of them do not even bother to check.

I show my cup to two other prisoners at the table, and they both check theirs. Not surprisingly, one of them also has a dirty cup. I encourage them to send request slips to the superintendent, complaining about the Food Services Department's lack of kitchen sanitation. When I get back to my housing unit later, I indeed send a request slip to the superintendent about this matter. I wonder if the other prisoners did so as well. Probably not.

Before I rise to leave, I slip a slice of bread into my pocket for my special friends. Then I pick up my tray and place it inside a small wall window, on the other side of which workers are removing leftover food and hastening each tray through a washing machine.

I always notice the vast amounts of food thrown out every day. At one time, prison officials at each institution knew what kinds of food to order and how much to prepare for a specific inmate populace, so there was little waste. Now, however, all institutions prepare the same menus, so inmates receive identical selections. Prisoners who do not want certain foods get them anyway, and unconsumed victuals are eventually thrown out. I think about the hundreds of thousands of Americans who may be hungry and malnourished at this moment, while prisons across the nation thoughtlessly waste so much food.

With that thought in mind, I exit the dining hall and go outside, back toward my housing unit. I try not to think about how I will be forced to repeat this same dreary routine day in and day out for many years to come.

*   *   *

Tonight, the dining hall is serving liver with beef gravy, probably the least favorite of all prisoners. The meal is served with two scoops of previously dehydrated mashed potatoes that are so dry and solidified that they could be used as paste to fill the holes in my cell walls. Green beans are also served, along with diced red beets and rehydrated onions, bread, oleo, and cherry-flavored drink. The meal smells bad and tastes bad. Before I pray over my supper, I wonder what there is on my tray to be thankful for.

Mr. Plum, a friend and a fellow lifer, joins me at my table. "Do me a favor and don't say anything," he says sarcastically. Mr. Plum and I came to SCI-Rockview a few days apart. Our friendship has gradually strengthened, but he sometimes gets annoyed at my constant "bitting."[1]

"What's the matter?" I ask him. "Is the food getting to you?"

"Yeah, I'm getting really tired of eating one bullsh** meal after another."

"Where do you think you are, the Holiday Inn?"

Mr. Plum smiles. "I knew you were going to say that."

I look back down at my tray and remember that the only reason I came to the dining hall was that I was still hungry from the meal before. My father always told me as a young boy to finish eating all the food on my plate, because there were people starving in other countries. Now, I feel like I am living in one of those countries. Sometimes, I would be very grateful to eat the scraps of real food that a dog is fed under the family table.

Rockview permits some of its prisoners to have one decent meal per year—at the annual banquet of inmate organizations inside the prison. Our Lifers' Association is one of them, and Mr. Plum and I are active members. The PLAR provides a formal banquet prepared and served by the Culinary Department. To be eligible to attend the banquet, a member must have attended at least six general membership meetings and be free of any class-one misconduct report[2] sanctions within the past six months. An eligible member may invite up to three guests, including family and friends. However, the prisoner must pay the entire cost of the meals for each guest.[3]

"Are you going to the Lifers' banquet?" I ask Mr. Plum.

"Yeah. My wife and mother will be coming up. What about you?"

I use my plastic fork to scrape off small pieces of unsavory onion clinging to my diced beets. "Yeah. My father, uncle, and a blind date."

"A blind date?" He looks at me as though waiting for some kind of punch line.

"I'm serious," I reply. "I haven't been in the company of a female for the past 11 years. I would like to have a date."

"You think some girl who doesn't know you will come in here on a blind date?"

"Why not? I'm a handsome guy."

Again, Mr. Plum smiles. By now, I have eaten a couple of spoonfuls of the mashed potatoes, most of the beets, two slices of stale bread, and the cherry drink. Although the meal lines are still serving, the dining room is not particularly crowded; an indication that tonight's meal is not very popular. As I turn in my tray at the window, I can see all the uneaten food left behind.

Mr. Plum and I leave the dining hall to return to our housing unit. I take advantage of the moment to do some bitting: "Tell me what I want to hear."

Caught off guard, he asks, "What's that?"

"Who's your daddy?" I ask jokingly in a deep, paternal register.

"Not you!" he immediately exclaims.

Despite all the negative conditions we endure, including our unpleasant dining experiences, we somehow find a way to avoid the sadness we encounter in our daily lives. Yet, no matter what we do as human beings to humor one another and cover up our true feelings, these stark realities haunt us every day.

Endnotes

1. A term used to indicate friendly joking at another's expense.
2. Class-one misconduct reports include serious infractions; class-two charges are considered less serious (e.g., horseplay, failure to report to work or school, smoking where prohibited, etc.).
3. Inmate organizations and their membership participation vary in each SCI, but in all of them, only a small percentage of the inmate population is eligible to attend an annual banquet. ✦

Chapter 6

The Commissary

The commissary is the prison store where inmates can purchase grocery items. It sells food, tobacco, cosmetics, and other types of general merchandise slightly below the product's suggested retail price. However, there are many items sold either at cost or slightly above. Each commissary product also has a mark-up of 5 percent, except for tobacco products which are marked up $.02 per package. The mark-up revenue goes to the Inmate General Welfare Fund (IGWF).[1]

In order for a prisoner to be able to make commissary purchases, he must first have sufficient funds in his institutional inmate account. Prisoners generally make deposits to their inmate account by earning monthly compensation from employment, attending school or other programs, receiving idle pay, or by having a civilian mail them a money order.

Prisoners may go to the commissary once every week. Each week, they are given a commissary order form that lists all the products that are sold in the store, including their prices. Commissaries at the different prisons basically sell the same type of products; however, the products' brands and prices may vary, depending on what vendor or distributor the institution contracts with. Over time, the prices of these products may go up at a faster rate than an inmate's compensation raises, thereby reducing his ability to purchase commissary items that are basic necessities.

A prisoner acquires a pass to go to the commissary on a specifically scheduled day, usually determined by what housing unit he is on or by the last digit in his prison identification number. Once he arrives, the Commissary officer punches in the prisoner's identification number to verify that he has sufficient funds to make pur-

35

chases. The officer then retrieves the items the inmate has marked off on his list. Prisoners can purchase only up to $45 worth of commissary products each week.

General products sold in the commissary include meat products, beverage/drink mixtures, candy, cookies, potato chips, pretzels, sugar, ice cream, soups, peanut butter, pies/cakes, coffee, tea bags, washcloths, towels, shaving products, toothpaste, toothbrushes, etc. Although some clothing items may be sold in the commissary, most of them must be purchased through an approved outside vendor via the mail. Electronic items (e.g., televisions, radios, typewriters, etc.) are now purchased through the commissary with a special order form.

If a product that the inmate has purchased is defective, he must contact the company that manufactured it if he wants a refund or an exchange. The commissary itself does not provide this service.

It can also be difficult for prisoners who work or attend school to go on their designated commissary day. They may have to seek access on a make-up day, since most work supervisors will not allow prisoners access to the commissary during work hours. Some prisoners prefer to purchase all the items they need for an entire month to prevent this situation.

*   *   *

I am sitting on my bed with my back to the cold concrete wall, reading a book, when a prisoner appears outside my cell and asks if I can spare "a shot of coffee."

Unless I know somebody really well, I will not accommodate anyone. I will simply tell the unwelcome guest that I have none to spare. Of course, I could offer a teaspoon of coffee, but I have learned from experience that if you give them your hand, they will inevitably come back for your arm. In prison, it is not about being or not being nice but about not letting your guard down to allow others to take advantage of you.

"Sorry, I can't spare any," I tell the stranger, annoyed that my reading has been interrupted. I hope he goes away and bothers someone else. Instead, the man looks around my cell, sees a container half full of sugar, and exclaims boldly, "Let me get some of that sugar!" Now I am angry. Perhaps he is just ignorant in matters of etiquette and respect, or maybe he is attempting a tactic of intimidation. Either way, he is not getting any of my sugar.

"No coffee, no sugar . . . and please don't ask me anymore," I respond, turning my attention back to the book. He finally gets the hint and leaves, but not without catching an attitude. Too bad it is not the same as catching a cold.

A common practice for prisoners is to place small signs next to their name tags on the front of their cell, warning other inmates not to ask for food, etc. It is quite effective as a deterrent. Others do not bother to hang a sign and have no problems saying no. There are those, however, who either out of kindness or for whatever reason, may give in to prisoners' requests for particular items.

Prisoners sometimes come to me, tell me they are hungry, and ask if I have anything to eat. To me, this is not a "want" but a "need." In cases such as this, I have no problem sharing some food that I might have. Going to bed hungry is a horrible feeling, so I always try to make sure that I have something for myself. And if I have enough to share with someone else, I will do so. The other person appreciates my kindness, and I feel good about being able to do it.

After the intruder is gone, I finish reading a chapter in my book, rise from my bed, grab my plastic cup, and make myself some coffee—sweetened with sugar.

*   *   *

"When the dining hall food sucks,
   and you're lucky enough to have a few bucks,
   go buy some food at the prison commissary,
   so you can make yourself a Chi Chi."

It was a hot summer night at Frackville. I cannot remember what they served for dinner, but like most prison meals, it was well worth forgetting. What I do remember, though, is how hungry I still was. I had no food in my cell and could not afford to borrow some. I was taking a shower, when I heard some of the other prisoners talking about tonight's nasty meal. Then I heard a voice remark, "Time for a Chi Chi."

I thought, a Chi Chi? What the hell is a Chi Chi? The stranger, who was Hispanic, said he could hook up a meal for us if we were willing to contribute. I have worked with some of the Hispanic prisoners in the Culinary Department, and I can tell you firsthand that they know how to prepare a good meal with even the lowest quality of food available.

That night after we were locked down for the evening, my Hispanic friend went to work cooking a meal for us. I had nothing to contribute but was promised a "breakdown," i.e., a small portion. When my portion arrived at my cell, it was more than enough to satisfy my hunger for the night.

Inside my cup was a mixture of noodles, rice, and chicken cooked with a variety of spices. I tasted a small spoonful of the Chi Chi. Much to my surprise, it was truly delicious.

You might ask, how does one cook anything at all in a prison cell? It is not easy. Some prisons provide what is commonly called a "hot shot" on the housing units: a special faucet that provides very hot, almost scalding water. Without a hot shot, prisoners either get mildly hot water from the sink in their cell, or they use a "stinger." Cooking with a stinger is very common in prisons across America.

A stinger is an electric cord with two pieces of metal attached to the end. They do not touch but are close enough to each other to heat up when dipped in water. The water itself is usually placed inside a washtub, and salt is added to help develop an electrical current. Too much or too little salt can blow a fuse, which means that other prisoners on the housing unit will also lose their electricity. Interfering with another inmate's TV or radio program can cause a serious problem.

Stingers have another drawback. When the electrical current moves through the submerged metal pieces, the metal corrodes and contaminates the water. So, meals are usually either cooked in an aluminum-lined bag (e.g., a potato chip bag) or in a plastic container that is immersed in the hot water. Stingers are prohibited by the Pennsylvania Department of Corrections. When a prisoner is caught with a stinger, mostly likely he will end up with a misconduct report for "possession of contraband."

Chi Chis have become very popular in the past few years. A prisoner familiar with cooking can create one, depending on what staples are available to him. Most Chi Chis are made by dissolving cheese curls into a soup, then adding Slim Jims or other types of meat that can be purchased in the commissary. When these items cannot be purchased, prisoners take food from the dining hall or kitchen, and smuggle them back to their cells.

Chi Chis traditionally are made on those days when the meals in the dining hall are unappetizing, or when they are able to shop at the commissary during pay week. It is certainly a treat, but it is also high in fats, cholesterols, and calories, which may cause a prisoner to gain weight. For those who can afford to make it, however, it is well worth the effort.

Recipe for a Traditional Chi Chi

(2) 3 oz. soup packages with seasoning
5 oz. cheese curls or cheese puffs
2 tbsp. cheese spread
1 handful of barbecue potato chips
2 Slim Jims or desired amount of meat

Add two cups of boiling (or very hot) water to the noodles, then cover for three minutes. Crush cheese curls and potato chips, then add the noodles when they are done. Add cheese spread and season packet, then mix until all ingredients are dissolved. Dice or cut meat as desired, then add to the Chi Chi. Enjoy.

Bof's Macaroni and Cheese

(4) 3 oz. soup packages with seasoning
5 oz. cheese curls or cheese puffs
4 oz. cheese spread
2 cups cheese crackers
2 oz. of regular cheese (if available)
10 oz. milk
2 tbsp. butter
1 cup desired meat

In a potato chip bag immersed in hot or boiling water, add milk, butter, and cheese spread first, then mix until these ingredients are dissolved evenly. Crush together the cheese puffs and cheese crackers, then add to the mixture in the bag. Mix these items together, until you are able to form a cheese sauce. Add more milk in order to get the desired effect of the sauce. If you add too much milk, simply add more crushed cheese curls. Add cheese, meat, and other desired seasonings (garlic, onion, pepper, etc.) along with the desired amount of soup seasoning packets. Stir evenly, then let stand for 20 minutes or until the cheese sauce mixture is hot. In a separate bowl or container, add eight cups of boiling or hot water to the dehydrated noodles, then let stand for three minutes or until the noodles are cooked. Drain the water from the noodles, then add the noodles to the cheese sauce, and mix evenly. Enjoy.

By the way, there is one more thing you might need: antacids.

Endnote

1. IGWF monies are generated by state prisoners and are used to purchase activities and recreational equipment (e.g., exercise machines, weight-lifting apparatus, sporting gear, etc.), inmate programs (art classes, concerts, music department, etc.), family resources (Read to a Child Program, etc.), visiting room (furniture, vending services, etc.), National Issues Forum, library (books, newspapers, magazines, etc.), and more, all of which significantly reduces the costs to taxpayers. The fund is administered by the prison officials. *See* Chapter 31 for an example of the IGWF buying tube socks to include in holiday packages for prisoners. ✦

Part III

Personal Hygiene

Chapter 7

Showers

I love soccer, one of the few sports that I actually enjoy playing. In prison, soccer can be a rough sport, especially with those who do not know what they are doing. It is 3 P.M. on a hot, humid day, and I am just returning from the yard after an exhausting game, during which my team won 4–2. My clothes are drenched with sweat and odor. All I can think about is getting out of these dirty, wet clothes and taking a shower.

In my cell, I strip down and put on a pair of clean boxer shorts to wear to the shower room. I dab some shampoo into my hair and leave behind the bottle, since it can easily be stolen from the shower room. I then wrap a washcloth around my soap dish, grab a clean T-shirt, and wear my white towel marked "COMM OF PA"[1] around my waist. Finally, I slip on a pair of rubber shower shoes that I have worn for the better part of three years.

I close and lock my cell, then I walk down the range to a flight of stairs that leads to a large iron gate, which at this particular time of day is open. I go through the gate to the front of the block, take a right, and proceed down the main corridor to the shower room in the center of the housing unit.

The shower room is not very crowded today, nor is my favorite showerhead being occupied. I quickly place my washcloth over it to indicate that it has been taken. In the middle of the shower room, there are metal racks with hooks for hanging clothes. I take an empty hook close to my showerhead, so I can keep an eye on my personal belongings. I put my glasses inside my T-shirt and hang it on the hook with my towel. Still in my boxer shorts, I return to my showerhead and drop my soap dish into the metal container that loosely hangs beneath it. I shift aside, turn on the water—already

43

warm, which means someone else just used it—then step into the steady flow.

I look around to see if there is anybody I know, friend or foe. Two showerheads over, a Puerto Rican comrade nods his head at me. I nod back, but we do not talk. Some men do not like talking in the showers, while others talk incessantly.

It takes me about 10 minutes to wash my entire body from head to toe. Today, the water is a bit hotter than normal, so I decide to stay under the shower a few minutes longer. I am in no hurry to get back to my cell.

For just a few moments, I try to escape the realities that surround me. I position my head directly under the shower to let the water pour over me. My eyes are closed, and it feels good to temporarily get away from it all. It feels so good. If there were no other inmates in the shower room, I might stay here for another 10 minutes. But more inmates are coming in, and I sense that it is becoming more crowded and noisier.

As with any inmate, security is my first priority. I turn off the shower, use my washcloth to wipe excess water off my body, then retrieve my glasses. I grab my towel, dry off, and don my T-shirt. Lastly, I tie my semi-wet towel around my waist and shake the remaining water from my shower shoes. There are puddles all around, so I walk carefully so as not to step in the dirty water. I do not always get my way, but today I manage to avoid these contaminated puddles.

Upon my return, I open my combination lock, enter my cell, and close the door behind me. Then I tie a piece of string on the bars so I can use my blanket as a privacy shield. This "curtain" is only temporary while I dry off and put on clean clothes. When finished, I take down the curtain and string. Sometimes, I go back downstairs for the remainder of the block-out period. Tonight, I hide underneath my bed linens and drift off to sleep until the evening meal line is called.

*   *   *

Obviously, every Pennsylvania prison has shower facilities. Unless a prisoner is receiving special medical treatment, however, soaking in a hot, bubbly bathtub is a benefit of freedom that we can only dream about. SCI-Huntingdon has two main shower rooms, each of which is used by two housing units at separate times. Each shower room has large pipes that travel across the ceiling dispensing regulated water streams from about 70 showerheads.

The shower room frequently becomes crowded, and inmates either have to wait for an open shower or share one with another inmate. Some refuse to share, since they regard their shower as private space, despite the fact that they are in a room of 50 to 80 men.

When the shower bell rings, you hear many doors opening and banging shut, many combination locks clicking, and the slapping footsteps of rubber shoes racing to the shower room. Some showerheads are better than others, so this race is rewarded with a first-come, first-serve prize. Although rare, an inmate may declare a certain showerhead to be exclusively his and, depending on how weak the competition is, may arrogantly tell someone to get out of "his" shower. But the unwritten code of conduct among prisoners is first come, first serve.

Another code of conduct is that inmates wear boxer shorts or briefs to the shower. Although most honor this rule, a few shower naked. Others consider this offensive: Men who shower naked are considered freaks, homosexuals, or disrespectful to others and themselves. But in all fairness, many feel more comfortable showering naked and claim it as a natural part of life.

It is not uncommon to observe a few inmates washing each other's backs, or even performing sexual acts in the shower room. Well aware that such behavior exists, most prisoners make an effort to keep their eyes on their own body.

In most of the older state prisons, showers run 10 to 15 minutes long, depending on the guard who is stationed at its post. During this time, it is essential that an inmate keep a close eye on his clothes, towel, or other shower items. The unobservant often fall prey to thieves, and occasionally an honest inmate picks up someone else's towel by mistake.

Shower rooms are annoying for other reasons. It is a small, enclosed area with a large number of prisoners, so it is often extremely noisy and overcrowded. An inmate can accidentally (or deliberately) bump into another inmate or splash some soap or water on him. The offended party can become aggravated, which may lead to a verbal confrontation or even an assault.

Furthermore, shower rooms have flat concrete floors covered with dirty puddles. Those walking by may splash soiled water on someone else, leading to yet another altercation. Another problem is the lack of water pressure or the staff's inability to maintain a proper water temperature. Guards who can control the temperature have been known to purposely make showers uncomfortable out of meanspiritedness.

At SCI-Rockview, the main housing units (the "wings") have larger shower rooms than those for smaller housing units (the "blocks"), but they are only about half the size of the shower rooms at SCI-Huntingdon. When I first arrived at Rockview in 1999, the shower rooms were often crowded, especially during the evening, and had only about 25 showerheads. There were about 400 prisoners on each of the two wings, and at least 300 of them wanted to shower during the course of a day. Because of the overcrowding, the shower rooms were eventually remodeled and now have between 60 and 70 showerheads. Even after such improvements, they still remain crowded from time to time.

At Rockview, sexual activity seems to be rare in the shower rooms, so inmates are less careful about keeping their eyes to themselves. On the other hand, a larger portion of inmates shower naked at Rockview than at Huntingdon. Contrary to popular belief, prisoners do not become sexually assaulted when they "drop the soap."

At SCI-Frackville, each housing unit has a section of four shower stalls where inmates can shower one at a time behind a closed plastic curtain. Those in the general population are able to shower once a day for a period of 10 minutes. Guards stand watch and usually give a two- or three-minute warning before one's time in the shower stall expires. Inmates who go beyond the time limit are often issued misconduct reports, especially when one violates the time limits more than once.

Though unusual, some state prisons assign female guards to observe showers, which can make both them and the male prisoners uncomfortable. At one point, an inmate purposely allowed the curtain to fall from its Velcro clasp while a female guard stood watch. The guard could have easily looked away, but instead looked directly at him, arousing laughter from other inmates. She gave the naked inmate a direct order to place a towel around his waist and go to his cell. The man was later seen handcuffed and taken to the RHU.

Endnote

1. Commonwealth of Pennsylvania. ✦

Chapter 8

Laundry

Returning to my cell after a long, hard day, I notice that the large brown paper bag that I use as a laundry basket is full of dirty clothes. The thought of cleaning my dirty laundry makes me feel more tired that I already am. All I want to do is to relax. I could put it off until tomorrow, I say to myself, but I know that tomorrow's schedule will not permit any procrastination on my part.

The easiest way to dispense with dirty clothes is to simply stuff them into a mesh bag and hand it in to the prison's Laundry Department twice a week for washing. Notice that I said "washing," not "cleaning." Imagine having your clothes washed with all the other inmates' laundry. A perfectly white T-shirt will almost always come back yellow.

Once, I submitted a grievance at Frackville because I had handed in a soiled pillowcase, only to have one returned that was just as dirty. The deputy superintendent who handled my grievance claimed that laundry procedures had met satisfactory standards. He knew my claim was legitimate, but as a loyal old soldier to the Pennsylvania Department of Corrections, he could not admit that Frackville was not properly cleaning our bed linens.

Later, I challenged the housing unit manager to a simple test. When the pillowcases came back from the laundry, I had her pick one out and hand it to me. Then I rewashed it in my clean washtub with a bar of Ivory soap bought from the commissary. I showed the unit manager how dirty the water was in my washtub. Her shocked reaction proved my point.

Another reason why some prisoners do not use the prison laundry is that inmates who work there often steal clothes. The institution will not assume responsibility for any lost or stolen items. To avoid unnecessary trouble, many prisoners simply wash their own clothes, as I do. I would rather scrub away in my cell with commissary-bought Ivory soap, or even the prison-made green Penncor soap, than risk losing clothes to theft or having them ruined by incompetence.

How does one wash clothes in a prison cell? First, I separate my white clothing (mostly underwear) from the colors (browns). My washtub is a cheap, plastic two-and-a-half–gallon container. After several uses, it tends to crack, forcing me to purchase a new one at the commissary every six months or so.

Using my small plastic drinking cup, I transfer hot water from my sink into the washtub. Taking one article of clothing at a time, I apply soap into the material, until it produces a lather. With rapid strokes, I then rub the pieces of clothing together, concentrating on the most soiled areas. I then ring as much water as I can out of the wet clothing, then dump the dirty soap water into the toilet and flush it down.

Again, I fill my washtub with more hot water from the sink. Placing my soapy clothing back into the washtub with clean water, I rinse them and repeat this cycle several times until every article is clean.

Hand laundering is very straining on the back, a fact that in itself motivates prisoners to just submit their clothes to the Laundry Department. For me, however, it is the sense of discipline and pride that keeps me going, despite the discomfort.

If one can afford to buy laundry detergent in the commissary, it makes the ritual that much easier. Soaking laundry overnight in a washtub full of Wisk also helps to get one's clothes clean. Most of us, though, cannot afford this small luxury.

*   *   *

In some Restrictive Housing Units, laundry becomes an even more difficult task, because RHU inmates have no access to the Laundry Department and *must* wash their own clothing. Although each prison's RHU is built differently, the flow of sink water is usually regulated in slow, small amounts like the water from a drinking fountain. To clean just three articles of clothing can take as much as an hour or two of hard labor. Most RHUs, however, provide a clothing-exchange type of service.

Some inmates in the RHU will first clean out their toilet, then proceed to wash their clothes in it. During my first time in the RHU in 1992, I thought that prisoners who did their laundry in the toilet were crazy. I could never imagine myself performing such a humiliating act. I would never stoop to such a level, so I thought. But soon tiring of the manual labor of sink laundry, I too found myself washing my laundry in the toilet. It was less frustrating and a whole lot easier.

Once, while in the RHU, I was washing my clothes in the toilet, when a nurse came to my cell to give me medication for a stomachache. She saw me sitting on the cold concrete floor with my soapy hands in the toilet and reacted with horror: "Don't you know that toilets have bacteria, germs, and viruses?!"

Somewhat embarrassed, I told the nurse, who was young and newly hired, that it takes too much time to wash my clothes in the sink. "With all due respect, ma'am, if you were forced to live in this cell, you'd probably do the same thing." She shook her head and walked away, but when the guard keyed the pothole closed, he just smiled at me. ✦

Chapter 9

Haircuts

Once a month, Pennsylvania prisoners are given the privilege of a haircut. All one has to do is submit a request slip, asking the Barber Shop supervisor to schedule an appointment. Most prisoners have no trouble getting their hair styled the way they want it.

Haircuts are not only a privilege but are mandatory. If a prisoner lets his hair grow too long, a guard or staff member will give him a direct order to get it cut. Prisoners who want to keep their hair long may petition the Pennsylvania Department of Corrections for haircut exemptions based on cultural or religious restrictions, as might a Native American or a Rastafarian. Proof of verification regarding cultural ancestry or religious background allows some inmates to wear long hair, though prison officials often frown on such claims as a form of manipulation. Staff members, especially guards, do not like prisoners wearing their hair over the shirt collar. In their view, long hair is a "security concern," though they have failed to convince the courts of such a claim.

In our view as prisoners, we believe that since most prison officials were former military personnel, they prefer inmates with regulation haircuts as a way of controlling their identity. Prisoners often try to take such identity control away from the staff, most often by manipulation. This usually angers prison personnel to the point that they tend to overly harass longhaired inmates.

We commonly believe that staff members need to have complete control over a prisoner, or their authority will be compromised. This effect on their authority, not the length of the hair itself, is what they believe to be a security concern.

* * *

Each day, a "Call-Out"[1] is placed on the housing unit's bulletin board to notify prisoners of their meetings or appointments (e.g., school, medical, barber shop, treatment program, gym, etc.). The bulletin board hangs about eight inches behind a rusty, steel-mesh fence that one has to peer through. I notice my name and number on the list: I am scheduled for the barbershop at 9:30 A.M.

When 9:30 A.M. arrives, I go to the "bubble"[2] to retrieve my pass. As I leave the housing unit, a small brown and white sparrow notices me and flies to a nearby fence less than six feet away. I know that the unit manager has asked me not to feed the birds. Although I respect his authority, I instinctively reach inside my coat pocket to find a few small breadcrumbs. The small bird watches me excitedly, as I surreptitiously throw the crumbs to the ground. Without hesitation, my little friend flies down to retrieve some nourishment.

It is a fairly nice day today. In the distance on the grass, I observe a male pigeon, all puffed up and walking in circles near a female in an apparent mating dance. As he ventures closer to the female, she hurriedly skitters away. The male chases after her to again impress himself upon her, but this time she seems on the verge of flying off. I resume my pace along the cracked concrete walkway towards the Education Building, hoping that the little guy gets lucky.

When I arrive at the Education Building, I hand the guard my ID card, show him my pass, then proceed to the barbershop. There an inmate takes my pass and gives me a green card with a history of my barber shop visits. When I check my card, it tells me that the last time I was here was two months ago.

I take off my coat and sit down on a wooden bench until a barber chair is open. The shop is normally crowded, but not today. An acquaintance of mine, a former fellow parateacher, motions me toward his chair. We greet each other, and I ask him for a very short cut with skin tapers on the sides. He sits me down, covers me with an apron, and proceeds with a pair of electric shears.

We talk briefly about his new job. He finds it more relaxing to be a barber than a parateacher. We reminisce on our accomplishments in the classroom. The topic changes to how the Department of Corrections has taken away almost every privilege we ever had, among them furloughs, holiday food visits, rehabilitative programs, and access to outside food-service vendors. We exchange sarcastic guesses as to what prison officials will take away from us next.

Life-sentenced prisoners in particular have undergone many new hardships, such as inmate organizational restrictions, losses of outside clearance status, ineligibility for reduced college tuitions and for attendance in various educational and rehabilitative programs, and denials of the viewings and funerals of deceased family members. With each passing year, we find ourselves losing many rights and privileges that previous lifers fought hard to establish in the 1970s and 1980s, thereby making prison life an even more difficult existence.

Occasionally, I look around at other prisoners waiting their turn for a haircut. Among them, an older man sits with his head down, looking depressed. I wonder if he is wishing he were home with his family. I hear soft-pop music coming from the radio at a low volume. Except for the old man, everyone else seems to be absorbed and content.

My barber and I speculate whether haircuts, like medical treatment, will eventually cost prisoners money. "Nah," I say sarcastically, "because if they (the Department of Corrections) did that, it would mean that prisoners could wear their hair as long as they want, and that would be a 'security concern.' "

When my haircut is finished, he hands me a mirror. In addition to my handsome features, I see that he has done an exceptionally good job and tell him so. A sign in the barbershop reminds patrons that tipping is not permitted, since the barbers are students and already receiving an hourly wage. However, some barbers avoid cutting a prisoner's hair unless he pays him a pack of cigarettes.

Although no one is obliged to pay for services that are provided by the Department of Corrections, in my view, prisoners can tip their barbers if they want to do so. As in the free world, if a barber does a good job, then it is customary to give him a tip, usually in the form of a commissary item like tobacco or candy. Due to my financial circumstances at this particular time, I cannot tip my barber. I let him know, however, that I will remember him the next time that I go to the commissary (a Snickers perhaps). I thank him, and we give each other a "pound,"[3] the prison equivalent of a handshake.

My barber signs the green card, which I take back to the inmate at the front desk. He gives my pass to the Barber Shop supervisor who marks the time that I am leaving, then hands it back. As I depart the Education Building, I retrieve my ID card from the guard sitting at the desk.

En route to the housing unit, a friend compliments me on my nice haircut.

"Thanks," I tell him. I wonder if that pigeon got as lucky as I did.

Endnotes

1. A daily list of inmates who will be "called out" of the block for specific purposes.
2. A glass-enclosed room that serves as the office for the guards.
3. Each person makes a fist, and the two fists are "pounded" together in a specific sequence of actions. ✦

Part IV

Medical Care

Chapter 10

A Visit to Medical

At 6 A.M., a loud bell shatters the peaceful silence. The guards make their daily rounds to count prisoners. Given that it is a mandatory standing count, I must turn on my cell light and remain standing on my feet, so that at least one of Pennsylvania's nearly 41,000 state prisoners can be accounted for.

As two guards pass by my cell, one stops to inform me that I have a mandatory medical pass at 8:30 A.M. I have no idea what I am being called for. Instead of worrying about it, I turn off my light and go back to bed before breakfast lines are called.

After breakfast, about five minutes before my scheduled appointment, I report to the bubble for my pass to the Medical Department. I must go through a gate to receive authorized entrance, so I show both my pass and ID card to the guard before being allowed to enter. As I make my way to the treatment building, I enter yet another door and again show my pass and ID card to a guard behind a second bubble. Once I am checked off a list, the guard keeps my ID card and pushes a button that electronically opens up a security door into the Medical Department lobby.

Inside the lobby, prisoners wait on wooden benches to receive medical attention. Another security door allows medical personnel to emerge and call prisoners into the inner corridor. I give the nurse my pass and find an open seat on the benches. A wall clock reads 8:34 A.M.

I occupy my waiting time talking to a prisoner acquaintance. He complains that the eye doctor rushed him through his eye examination a few months back, then he had to wait 11 weeks to receive a new pair of glasses. The glasses he received did not correct his vision, so he had to file a grievance against the Medical Department.

They initially denied his grievance, until he appealed to the super-intendent, who ordered Medical to correct the problem. That was three weeks ago. A great number of complaints from prisoners relate to medical treatment.

8:56 A.M.

A long line of diabetic prisoners waits to receive their finger tests. Most of them are older prisoners, a few supported by walking canes. I notice various wall posters promoting good dietary habits and advice on how to quit smoking. One in particular stresses the importance of eating from the four basic food groups, displaying various fruits, vegetables, meats, and other wholesome foods that make my mouth water. I consider asking the nurse if I could send this poster to the Food Services manager, hoping to give him a better idea of what the food he serves should look like.

Through a set of windows, we can see people walking through the inner corridor; most of us are trying to catch glimpses of the female nurses. Some of them are quite attractive, while others are plain. To men who have "been down" for as much time as myself, even the most unappealing female can look ravishing.

My attention returns to the clock, minutes ticking by like hours. Though sometimes an inmate can get quick medical treatment, it is more common to spend from 45 minutes to two hours just waiting. In other institutions, it is even worse.

9:18 A.M.

A nurse opens the security door and calls out "BQ-3769," my identification number. I think to myself, because of some unknown summons I have to wait 43 minutes on a hard bench only to be re-minded that both my identity and dignity have been stripped away from me. But I try to dismiss this small aspect of the dehumaniza-tion process. As I approach the nurse, she asks, "Are you BQ-3769?"

"That's only my ID number," I reply with an ironic smile. "You can call me Mr. Paluch."

She leads me into the Medical Department corridor and over to a weight scale against the wall. I step onto it: 196 pounds. I am then escorted down the corridor to an examination room where a female Physicians Assistant (PA) awaits me.

* * *

The PA tells me that I have been summoned for my biannual physical. She would like to ask me some questions. As I answer them, I cannot help but notice that she is more attractive than most of the other female nurses. She uses a small light to check my eyes, mouth, nose, and ears, then places a stethoscope to my chest and back. She then asks me to do some various reflex exercises and walking patterns, then fingers my neck for swollen glands.

Finishing off, she dons a pair of rubber gloves. "The next part of this test is very important. Now that you're 30 years of age, you should have both your testicles and prostate checked for signs of—"

I interrupt her. "Are you asking me to remove my pants?"

"Yeah."

I explain that I feel very uncomfortable revealing my private parts to strangers, especially a female, and I would be more comfortable with a male PA.

"Well, okay," she replies, "but you should make sure that you check yourself for any lumps or unusual pains. You're going to have to sign a waiver stating that you refused to be examined for this test." She hands me a waiver, which I read, sign, and date. Before leaving, I request an appointment to have my ears flushed to remove any excess earwax. She signs my pass, and I wish her a good day.

A few days later, I return to the Medical Department to get my ears flushed. I also undergo a hearing test, then give blood and urine samples. Other than the long lobby wait, I appreciate the fact that I was provided a free physical, especially since there are many people in free society who cannot afford such a privilege.

* * *

In 1998, the Pennsylvania General Assembly passed a law described as "Inmate Medical Co-Pay." This law requires that all prisoners pay two dollars for nonemergency medical services provided at the inmates' request, including those for self-inflicted injuries and injuries sustained from a prisoner's assaultive conduct. This also includes treatment for sports-related injuries and for medical examinations an inmate needs to be approved to play a sport. Charges are also incurred when the Medical Department provides an initial prescription medication.

Prisoners are not charged for follow-up medical services, physicals, annual dental examinations, mental health treatment, eyeglass exams (provided biannually) or prescriptions, and a host of other medical services. No inmate is refused medical services or treatment for financial reasons, but a prisoner's account will be debited as soon as he acquires sufficient funds.

To working people in the free world, this does not sound like a bad deal. However, a majority of prisoners do not have jobs. If they do, they have to work about 10 hours in order to earn the two dollars needed to pay for medical services. Hence, many inmates often do not seek the medical care they genuinely need out of fear of losing hard-earned dollars.

Legally, this would not seem to be a problem. The U.S. Supreme Court has held that prisons must provide "minimally adequate medical care to those whom they are punishing by incarceration." However, prison officials are allowed to set their own guidelines as to what constitutes "minimally adequate medical care."

Prisoners who experience chronic or long-term diseases suffer the most from "minimally adequate medical care." Although medical services and treatment are provided, such remedies are not always the most effective methods of available treatment. Prescription medications may be either generic or over-the-counter brands, while more effective medications may be denied simply because they are too expensive. Surgeries and operations that require transferring a prisoner to an outside hospital are severely limited or restricted.

Prisoners who suffer from hepatitis C, cirrhosis, and severe liver damage (even requiring a liver transplant) are simply out of luck. They are placed last on the list of those eligible for an available organ. Older and infirm prisoners are frequently neglected when it comes to medical needs, especially lifers and other long-term offenders who may be without family members or friends to advocate for them.

In addition, prisoners have no way of knowing if the medical services provider is licensed or qualified to provide such services. Numerous cases are known of prison doctors, specialists, and nurses who were dismissed because they were not licensed to practice medicine. Medical personnel, who either lost their licenses or were suspended due to malpractice, are often hired to work inside prisons as a probationary means to reinstate their licenses. Numerous cases have occurred in which doctors failed to properly diagnose illnesses or medical problems. Prisoners often file malpractice lawsuits against medical personnel. Although the courts have made it extremely difficult for prisoners to prove claims of medical negligence, there are a few cases in which they did win their lawsuits or defendants agreed to settle out of court.

Most medical personnel are professional and courteous to their patients, willing to give them the best care and treatment, but others are less willing. If there is one thing a prisoner dislikes, it is a rude, arrogant, or uncaring staff member, including medical personnel. On the other hand, medical staff members may have to deal with prisoners who act rude or display a poor attitude towards them, many who have terrible hygiene, bad breath, and a host of health disorders. In addition, female medical personnel are frequently subjected to sexual harassment by prisoners, especially sexual offenders.

Many doctors, specialists, nurses, and other medical personnel have witnessed for themselves the inadequacies of medical treatment received by prisoners, but their power to correct these problems is limited by both the PA DOC and the contracted health-care provider's policies and regulations that govern them.

One nurse at Rockview told me, "I know about all the politics which are played against (you) inmates. It's not that we don't care, but that we can only do what we are permitted to do. We are literally handcuffed by the prison administrators and by health-care provider officials."

When I asked this nurse why she continued to work for such an inadequate medical system, she replied, "It's hard to get as good a job anywhere else. They pay me very well, and the benefits that come with the job are superior compared to other jobs."

Medical care and treatment inside Pennsylvania's prisons have improved over the past decade, mainly due to inmate lawsuits. People in the free world often complain about prisoners who file lawsuits. However, if we did not have access to the courts for redress, we would be in far worse shape than we presently are.

It is estimated that about 25 percent of Pennsylvania's nearly 41,000 prisoners are infected with hepatitis C. Diseases such as HIV continue to spread behind bars as they do in the free world. The United States needs to provide adequate health services for its incarcerated population, despite the fact that prisoners are viewed as the lowest class of U.S. citizens. ✦

Chapter 11

A Painful Experience

B ecoming sick in prison can be a dangerous experience. I have seen countless prisoners contract serious diseases, such as cancer, HIV, and various types of hepatitis. Instead of healing, more often they grow sicker and weaker. Prisoners with such injuries as broken bones are not always given the proper medical treatment and frequently develop complications and other chronic ailments.

When I first arrived at SCI-Huntingdon, I witnessed the collapse of an elderly prisoner as he hurried to the pill line to receive his medication. He fell over headfirst onto the cold cement floor in front of my cell. When he did not respond to my calls, I yelled to the guards for help. No one came. Half a minute went by, when another prisoner passed by my cell. I quickly told him to alert the guards that the fallen inmate needed medical attention. A minute later, a guard stopped to observe the prostrate elder. I urged him frantically to call the Medical Department.

As I waited for help, I noticed the old man's vacant, open eyes and stiff face. Three minutes later, a nurse approached at a leisurely pace with a small green tank on wheels. She checked the man's wrist for a pulse then said, "I think he's dead."

About five minutes later, the body was removed. I subsequently learned that the old man, a lifer, had died of a heart attack.

I have personally seen too many of these horrors and heard about too many others. When my o'heads tell me to take good care of my physical and mental health, I know they speak from experience.

I exercise both body and mind on a daily basis and consume a daily dose of multivitamins purchased from the prison commissary—all in a desperate effort to prevent illness. But I cannot prevent the harrowing experience that one night invaded my body and threatened my life.

*   *   *

It is a Saturday night. My housing unit is secured and we are locked inside our cells. After my Sabbath prayers, I decide to relax and watch some television before going to bed. One of my favorite shows, *All In The Family,* is on, which I tune in to get a few laughs. In the middle of the show, I begin to suffer a stomachache. I find some Rolaids and take two tablets. The peppermint flavor makes me sneeze as usual, but this time it hurts when I sneeze. However, I dismiss any notion that something might be seriously wrong.

The stomach pains worsen, so I take a few more Rolaids, turn off the television, and go to sleep. About two o'clock in the morning, I wake up with excruciating pain in my abdomen. Again, I take more antacids and try to go back to sleep, wondering why the Rolaids are not kicking in.

By 3 A.M., the pain grows unbearable. I begin to vomit. Barely making it to my cell door, I call out for the night guard on duty. It takes a couple of yells before he finally comes around.

"What's the problem?" he inquires.

"I've got awful stomach pains, and I'm vomiting. I need medical attention."

The guard walks away without a word. Hopefully, he has gone back to the bubble to telephone the Medical Department nurse. A few minutes go by before he returns.

"I called the nurse," he reports, "and they're going to put you on the list for sick call."

Sick call is operated inside each state institution every Monday through Friday. Prisoners can sign up by filling out a form. Except for emergencies or follow-ups, an inmate must pay an initial fee of $2.00. After he signs a Cash Slip,[1] he can then be screened by a Physician's Assistant. Today is Sunday. I would have to wait another day to see the PA. I cannot wait that long.

"I've got to see a doctor now," I beg the guard. "I'm in a lot of pain, and something is wrong."

The guard tells me there is nothing more he can do and walks away.

At this point, the vomiting reoccurs at 10-minute intervals. I dampen a washrag and wipe my face. I am now beginning to sweat, though I cannot sense any fever.

I do not remember how I ended up on my cell floor. I must have passed out. My body is too weak to rise. I need more help than I previously thought. Single-cell prisoners usually have a code signal in times of emergencies: a cell lock is banged on the wall to alert one's neighbor. But my lock is hanging just above the sink, and I cannot reach it. On a nearby chair lies my shoe brush. I grab it and start banging on the wall, too weak to do so loudly. Minutes pass before my cell neighbor awakens.

"What's going on?" he asks.

"I need help," I answer, but he does not hear me. I bang on the wall again.

"What's the matter?"

"I need help!" I call out as loudly as I can.

"CO,[2] we've got a man down in 256 cell!" my neighbor shouts. "CO, we've got a man down!"

Another guard finally appears, sees me on the floor, and asks me what the problem is.

"I need to see a doctor," I reply. "I'm sick, and I already passed out. Please get me some help!"

At about 4:30 A.M., a male nurse arrives to check on me. By now, my lower abdominal region is intensely painful, and the right side of my stomach feels hot. I show him the vomit inside my toilet. He also sees that I am sweating, yet I have no fever. He takes my blood pressure. It appears to be normal.

"I think you've got the flu," he assumes.

"It's not the flu," I assure him. "I know what the flu is like. Something is wrong, and I need to see a doctor."

"The doctor won't be in until later this morning."

"Can't you at least send me to the infirmary?"

"That's not going to happen. I'll put you on the list to see the doctor in the morning. Until then, try to get some rest."

Shortly after the nurse leaves, I begin to throw up a nasty-tasting, greenish-yellow liquid—my bile. Before I can make it back to my bed, I pass out again.

* * *

The 6:00 A.M. bell rings for standing count. I stagger to my door and yell for the guard.

"What's the problem, Mr. Paluch?" The same damned question.

"Something is terribly wrong. I need to see a doctor. I don't think I'm going to make it."

The guard promises to see what she can do. I am too weak to stand for count. I collapse on my bed then vomit for the umpteenth time.

The sergeant on duty comes to my cell to inform me that the Medical Department was contacted, and I should expect to see the doctor between 8 and 9 o'clock. I do not think I can last that long.

The bell rings again for 7 o'clock breakfast lines. I make a half-hearted attempt to get dressed. There is no way I can eat anything, but I need some fresh air. As I drag myself down the tier, I begin to hiccup profusely. I make it to the dining hall, give my tray to another prisoner, then leave. Before I can make it back to my housing unit, I vomit on the walkway grass.

I make it back to my cell. I am not sure exactly what happens next. I wake up and find myself on my cell floor again. The sergeant is calling my name.

"Listen, I called the Medical Department again. They don't want me to send you down there. They called the doctor, and he's expected to come in shortly. Hang on, buddy."

From time to time, the sergeant returns to my cell. He has not heard anything yet. I vomit my bile again and again.

"Please get me to a hospital," I cry out plaintively. "I need help!"

*   *   *

Another three hours will pass before I am helped off the cell floor by a fellow prisoner and taken to the Medical Department. At 12:00 noon, he literally carries me to the treatment building. Once inside the medical lobby, it will be another 15 minutes before a nurse attends to me.

The nurse suggests it might be food poisoning. She wants to admit me to the prison infirmary, but the infirmary guard refuses my admission, because he says that it will "interfere with the count."

I sit in the cold medical lobby, vomiting and shivering for two more hours before a doctor arrives at Rockview. Another agonizing 15 minutes eke by before he examines me.

"It's probably food poisoning," the doctor assumes. "I'm going to admit you to the infirmary, place you on intravenous fluids, and give you some medication for the pain and to relax your insides."

I remain in the infirmary for the rest of the day and overnight. The pain in my abdominal area does not cease, but the vomiting and sweating stop. The following morning, the regular institutional doctor examines me. He is not sure what the problem is, but I convince him that I need to get to a hospital.

Another nurse visits my room, feels my stomach region, and determines that I have appendicitis. "I've seen this before, and I'm pretty sure that's what you've got."

* * *

At two o'clock that Monday afternoon, I begin my journey to a hospital in a town about an hour away. I am admitted through the emergency room, but it is not until 6:30 P.M. that I receive a CAT scan. Three hours later, a hospital doctor diagnoses me with acute appendicitis and orders me to stay in the hospital overnight for surgery the following morning.

"I've been working all day, and I'm tired," says the doctor. "I'm going to place you on some antibiotics which will hopefully slow the process until your appendix is removed."

I ask the doctor if I can be given some food, since I have not eaten since 5 P.M. on Saturday, almost two days ago. He agrees that I can. The two guards from Rockview who brought me to the hospital wait until a guard from SCI-Cresson comes to watch me. A kind nurse brings me a peanut butter-and-jelly sandwich, mini-wheat cereal, a small cup of sherbet, and a lemon-lime soda. I eat my food in a hospital bed with my right leg shackled to its side post. An elderly guard from SCI-Cresson warily watches over me.

The following morning, I wash up in preparation for surgery. At 12 P.M., I am wheeled into a room where an anesthesiologist sets to work. Before she puts me to sleep, I tell him a joke about a duck that walks into a bar and asks for something to eat. As the anesthesiologist rests a plastic cup over my nose and mouth, I say a silent prayer to Yahweh. I once had surgery for a hernia repair while I was at SCI-Frackville in 1998. When I was put to sleep, I was not even aware that I was unaware of anything. There was no mental pain, no noise—nothing! Only peace. This is what I ask Yahweh for in my prayer now.

The surgery goes well. I stay overnight in the hospital on the doctor's orders, even though SCI-Rockview wants to bring me back to the prison. Rockview's Medical Department is under contract to a private medical-services provider that controls the standards and quality of health care that state prisoners receive there. The less money this company has to spend on prisoner patients, the more profit it will gain.

In contrast to the treatment that I received at SCI-Rockview, I am fortunate to have the best hospital care. Although my medical condition remains painful, I am blessed with a cordial hospital staff that treats me with pleasant conversation and mutual respect. The meals are a treat—a release from the ordinary pangs suffered from prison food. Most of all, I will never forget the wonderful taste of human kindness offered during my stay at the hospital. It is more than I have ever felt in all the years that I have been incarcerated. On my trip back to the prison, I feel like crying.

When I return to Rockview, I am placed in the prison infirmary until the facility's doctor can see me the following morning. Inside the window of the infirmary's bubble is a sign that reads:

> *If you are a housed inmate living in this infirmary:*
>
> *DO NOT use your call bell to speak to a nurse.*
>
> *DO NOT use your call bell to request ice water.*
>
> *DO NOT ask for special favors.*
>
> *DO NOT bother the nurse when she/he is obviously extremely busy (unless it is a true emergency situation).*
>
> *DO NOT call the nurse for another inmate when he can do it for himself.*

I wonder if the hospital I just visited would ever put up such a sign for their patients. Mostly, I wonder about the fact that I enjoyed being put to sleep. If the life imprisonment I am serving now is meant to keep me incarcerated until I die, then why did Pennsylvania allow some doctor to save my life? If putting me to sleep permanently satisfies society's need to exact vengeance for my crime, as well as satisfying my quest for peace and happiness, then why was I given a second chance to live? Is it because society wants to see me suffer? I wonder.

As of this writing, I am still experiencing some pain and soreness from the surgery, not to mention some mental soreness towards the prison's Medical Department for treating me the way they did. I have filed a formal grievance, and the only relief I request from SCI-Rockview is that no future prisoner ever has to experience what I did. When such emergency situations arise, prisoners should be provided with proper medical attention and care within a reasonable amount of time.[3]

Had my appendix burst, I would have had peritonitis, a poisoning of the body that can result in death. Had I been in the prison infirmary instead of lying on a cold, dirty cell floor when my appendix burst, I would have had a better chance of surviving the ordeal. Had I been on the cell floor unconscious when my appendix ruptured, I would not be alive today to tell you my tale. But in society's eyes, perhaps that would have been a good thing.

Endnotes

1. A deduction from an inmate's account.
2. "CO" is used by prisoners and staff as a shortened version of "Correctional Officer," the proper title of a guard.
3. SCI-Rockview Medical Department denied any negligence or wrongdoing. Mr. Paluch appealed the grievance to the superintendent, who acknowledged that the medical staff should have provided more prompt treatment. ✦

Part V
Sex

Chapter 12

Sex in Prison

Prisoners deal with sexual deprivation in four possible ways.

1. *Abstinence,* the act of deliberately restraining from all sexual activity. This includes restraint from normal sexual relations, masturbation, or homosexual relations. Total abstinence is extremely rare among prisoners. I would estimate that perhaps one out of every 500 inmates actually has the will power to achieve total abstinence. Although some prisoners make honest attempts at self-restraint, they almost always find that human nature overpowers their efforts.

2. *Heterosexual relations.* Although heterosexual relations are prohibited in prison, they occur more frequently than an outsider may think. The most common occasion for heterosexual relations is with prison personnel in private encounters. For male prisoners, the opportunity may arise when a female staff person (a guard, nurse, librarian, culinary worker, etc.) has frequent social contact with a particular inmate. Sometimes, over the course of such contact, the female staffer becomes friendly with the inmate and engages in what might be called flirtatious behavior, including affectionate words or even gentle touching.

The male inmate tends to interpret these events as signals and, without concern for the possible consequences, may act on them. Most often, his ability to interpret these signals is distorted by virtue of his own deprived sexual appetite. If he is not careful, he may misinterpret an innocent act by the female, make a sexual advance toward her, and then find himself in the "the hole" (RHU).

When a male inmate is able to achieve a sexual relationship with a female staff person, the encounter may either be a one-time affair or may develop into a long-term relationship. It is unwise for any inmate to reveal or openly talk about sexual relations with a staff member to another inmate, since the latter may become jealous and reveal the affair to prison authorities, thus putting an end to it.

Prison officials normally do not publicize cases of their personnel caught in a sexual tryst with inmates, but I have heard one estimate that an average of 20 staff members a year in the PA DOC alone are either suspended or terminated from their job because of such sexual activity. Although rare, relations between prison personnel and inmates may result in a pregnancy, a continuing relationship, and even marriage.

Although I am not personally familiar with the sexual relations that exist between female prisoners and male personnel, it has been reported that male staff members have a greater tendency to exploit female prisoners for sexual favors, and that sexual assault, rape, and pregnancies do occur inside state prisons designed for women.

3. *Masturbation.* Without a doubt, this is the most common method of sexual gratification. It is also the safest alternative to direct sexual contact. For the majority of inmates, masturbation is performed in privacy, usually at night before going to bed.

Most prisoners do not openly talk about masturbation, as it is deemed a very private matter. However, an inmate may talk about the subject briefly with another close friend in whom they confide their thoughts.

For example, one inmate confided to me that when he "first fell" (a common prison phrase that means the time after an arrest, trial, and conviction), he would not masturbate while another inmate was in the cell with him. As time went on, he became frustrated because his celly was forever present, thus diminishing his time for privacy. So he got to the point where he would wait until his celly would go to bed before he could "get a good one off." "It's humiliating for me," he complained.

Although masturbation is considered by psychologists to be a normal behavior, religious inmates preach that it is a sin. I disagree. In my reading of the Holy Scriptures, nowhere in the Bible does it deal with the subject of masturbation. A religious inmate may tell you that one is not able to masturbate without having lust (another sin) for the person whom one fantasizes about. This could be true. However, if an inmate masturbates while thinking of his wife, would that still be a sin? I think not.

Very few inmates are married, and the majority of inmates who masturbate fantasize about another person with whom they have had or would like to have sexual relations with. For a male prisoner, a fantasy can become as lustful and creative as one's imagination is willing to take him. Whether it is a sin or not, masturbation is the most common method of dealing with forced sexual deprivation.

4. *Homosexual relations.* For many inmates, abstinence, hetero-sexual relations, and masturbation are either not options or are not satisfying alternatives to dealing with deprivation. Homosexuality exists in every prison across the state and the nation. In some prisons, it is more rampant than in others. Most homosexual relations in prisons are engaged in privately between consenting cellmates or between lovers in a place that is the least occupied by other inmates (a cell, bathroom, etc.), especially in places concealed from staff members. Of those who engage in such relations, some are openly gay, and a few will actually alter their personal appearance to make themselves resemble the opposite sex.

An acquaintance of mine who indulges in homosexual behavior admitted to me that he had "been down" so long that he became psychologically weak enough to try it out. His first experience was with a cellmate who convinced him that homosexual activity was "the next best thing to having the real thing." Ironically, my friend does not view himself as homosexual, since he is the "giver" and not the "receiver." When I asked him if he worried about HIV or hepatitis, he responded: "The kid (referring to his partner) seems clean. Besides, I'm doing 17 and a half to 35 years. I'm gonna die of something, anyway."

Although both white and African-American prisoners succumb to the experiences of homosexuality, it is often the young, baby-faced white inmates who are psychologically preyed upon, and who willingly submit to such activity either out of the need for protection or because they want to. Many young white inmates come to prison with deep-seated fears about what will happen to them there. Homosexual predators know this, and when they sense the young man's fear they play upon it, using psychological tactics to convince a newcomer that he needs protection and so on.

These victims who voluntarily agree to sexual relationships are looked upon by heterosexual prisoners as punks, faggots, b**ches, and "boys." When one is given a specific label that reflects one's reputation as a prisoner, it often stays with one for the duration of his incarceration. Interestingly enough, the Pennsylvania Department of Corrections does not teach young inmates this truth as an effective prevention-awareness method. The fact is that a large majority of inmates view homosexuality as immoral and deplorable. For most male prisoners, it degrades the very definition and essence of a man.

* * *

The following are some prisoners' reflections on masturbation:

Call me crazy, but I do it. As far as I'm concerned, everybody does. I'm in prison. I can't get any pussy so I gotta do what a man's gotta do—get it? I mostly think about my ex-girlfriends or some of their girlfriends who wish they could have me. Sometimes, I even fantasize about gettin' it on with two girls at once.

Yeah, I beat my dick. I don't play no games either! When duty calls, I get myself a smut book, slap a handful of body lotion on it, and I go to town. That's it.

First, I gotta have privacy. If there ain't no privacy, I ain't doin' it. And I don't do it if my celly is in the damn cell. I just close my eyes and think about some beautiful girls, mainly models, television stars, or singers. Occasionally, I think about a female guard or nurse.

I handle my business very well, thank you. I'm not proud of having to do this, but when nature calls, my body listens.

An old man like me no longer has a use for it.

Yeah, we lonely women do it, too. And when we can find an intimate partner, we do it to each other.

For the majority of prisoners, masturbation is both a private subject and a regular activity. Most prisoners refuse to talk about it either because they are too embarrassed or they feel it is nobody's business but their own. From time to time, I hear others joke about it. Yet for everybody here, sexual needs are a reality that human nature will not allow us to escape. Whether one performs his own personal ritual or tries to control his desires and urges for long periods of time, masturbation is a fact of life for the large majority of prisoners.

The act is usually performed at night before going to sleep, but it can also be done at any time of the day. For some prisoners, that would usually be during private moments when their cellmate is out of the cell. Most frequently, masturbation is performed alone, but there are a few cases where cellmates perform the act together. Rarely does a guard catch two inmates in the act, but it does happen.

In some prisons, it is quite difficult to masturbate, especially during the day. The prisoner may hang a towel on his door or try to hide behind linens on a clothesline. But prison officials severely restrict the privacy of prisoners. A hanging towel or linens in a cell can result in warnings or misconduct reports. Such restrictions are deep frustrations for inmates who need privacy to deal appropriately with their natural sexual needs.

For many lifers and long-term prisoners, masturbation becomes tedious over the years. This leads to attempts to stimulate new sexual fantasies to relieve the tedium. But the opportunities to do so are limited. The Pennsylvania Department of Corrections no longer allows its prisoners to receive naked photographs of their spouses or loved ones through the mail. Visual stimulation is limited to "soft" pornography in "approved" magazines (e.g., *Playboy,* etc.). In addition, a new DOC rule prohibits inmates from displaying nude centerfolds on their cell walls without covering up or opaquing out the girl's private parts.

All these restrictions may indirectly force a prisoner to experiment with homosexuality. One lifer told me, "I beat my dick for 15 years. I got tired of that." For him and for many others, homosexuality became a reality when masturbation was no longer able to satisfy their sexual desires.

* * *

He is very young. Never before has he been in a state prison. He has lived recklessly in society as a tough little man, until a judge sentenced him to a different world where his fears will confront him. He has heard the stories and rumors about prison life. He knows that if he shows any sign of weakness, the vultures who await him will make him their victim.

I know he is scared when I first see him carrying two boxes of personal effects into his new cell. I know what is going through his mind. I once thought the same way when I first ventured into this different world environment.

So I approach him. "What's your name, kid? Where ya from?" To him, I am a stranger. Perhaps he will see me as a friend, trying to give him some good advice. I tell him that if he needs any help, just let me know. To ease his mind, I assure him that I am not a homosexual. He will soon find out that a lot of prisoners will want to be his "friend." I bid him farewell, then go about my business.

The days go by, and I watch the vultures circle their prey. These parasites can never fulfill their desires for a beautiful woman, so an attractive young boy becomes the next best thing. This young boy now has become "the next best thing."

I want so much to go to him and let him know which inmates are the vultures. However, I learned my lesson a few years back when another boy told a vulture what I had said about him. I was fortunate enough to escape an assault. Minding one's own business in prison is a key element in maintaining good relations and avoiding assaults. Perhaps this boy is intelligent enough to quit hanging around his newfound friends. But I must admit, it pains me deeply to watch him slowly succumb to the degradation that awaits him.

My worst fears are realized when I hear that the young boy and a vulture have received the prison's approval to cohabit in the same cell. The vulture has succeeded in manipulating the youth's weaknesses and vulnerabilities. Perhaps he promised him protection, a television, a radio, or commissary gifts. Perhaps nothing was promised, and the vulture intends to gradually convince the boy that, in exchange for protection or commerce, he will be obligated to him. This psychological game is used by some prisoners as a way to thwart their sexual frustrations. Although the Pennsylvania Department of Corrections claims that it frowns on such behaviors, prison guards and administrators are very much aware of it and even tolerate it. Depending on what institution a prisoner is incarcerated in, prison officials often turn a blind eye when they see a young boy celled up with a vulture.

Most vultures are either long-term offenders or those who have been convicted of sexual offenses. Some rapists and child molesters come to prison only to victimize others in order to satisfy their disturbing behavioral patterns. By contrast, very few lifers are known to indulge in homosexual behaviors, although it does occur.

The last time I saw this young boy, he was sitting at the same table across from me in the dining hall. We did not speak to one another. After all, we have nothing in common. ✦

Chapter 13

Forced Sexual Deprivation

> Sex is natural, sex is fun,
> Sex is best when it's one-on-one.
> —George Michael, *I Want Your Sex*

When the song *I Want Your Sex* first came out, I was just 16 years old. The lyrics caused a lot of controversy at the time. I like the song, not because it is controversial, but because it is truthful. Michael's song speaks of the realities of our need for sexual relations. He also makes an important point when he sings, *Not everybody does it, but everybody should.*

Like eating and sleeping, sex is a natural act. It releases frustration, stress, and physical tensions, at the same time providing us with heightened pleasures. It consummates a marriage and produces offspring. When a human being is deprived of normal sexual relations, it interferes with his or her normal development process and contributes to an outbreak of emotional disorders.

I believe that sexual relations should not be classified as a right or a privilege, but as a human necessity.

For Pennsylvania prisoners, sexual relations are strictly prohibited. This forced deprivation in prison may seem like a suitable punishment for criminals, but is it? It has often been pointed out that citizens who commit crimes are sent to prison as punishment, not necessarily to be punished. That is, being imprisoned is itself the punishment. Denying an incarcerated person a basic and normal human need is an additional punishment beyond the experience of imprisonment itself.

In my view, the additional punishment of sexual deprivation interferes with society's attempt to rehabilitate the offender. In fact, it produces an adverse effect on the lives of most prisoners that can cause harmful consequences to both the prisoner and to society. In particular, it harms marriages, even though maintaining and supporting marriage is beneficial to both inmate and society.

It is very difficult for prisoners who are married to maintain meaningful relationships with spouses left behind in the free world. Both partners become susceptible to a sense of helplessness. Deprived of marital sex, each spouse is vulnerable to loneliness, which can lead to homosexual relationships for the incarcerated spouse and adultery for the free spouse. If both spouses are not strongly and faithfully committed to one another, " 'til death do us part," the marriage will slowly but inexorably move toward the finality of divorce.

There is no question that both spouses need the emotional, spiritual, and even physical experiences provided by the relationship in order for the marriage to survive. But these experiences are severely restricted.

During visits, even small displays of affection are forbidden. One kiss is permitted at the beginning and one kiss at the end of the visit. Physical contact is limited to holding hands or softly hugging the spouse's arm and shoulder.[1] No other displays of affection are allowed. There is absolutely no privacy in the visiting room, so any act of physical contact can be seen and heard by guards.

The length of an incarcerated spouse's sentence plays a major role in determining whether a marriage is going to survive the test of time. The free spouse may eventually realize that he or she is being unfairly burdened by the obligation to provide for all the needs of the incarcerated spouse when he or she is not receiving those same needs in return. A free spouse is also burdened with handling financial responsibilities (e.g., employment, children, bills, etc.) that the incarcerated spouse cannot reasonably assist with while in prison.

Even inmates who do everything within their limited power to save their marriage often end up facing divorce. For lifers and other long-term offenders, the percentage of marriages that end in divorce is even higher. Unless both spouses are willing to sacrifice and dedicate their lives to each other, the marriage is likely to fail.

There are very few cases in which marriages continue to work while a spouse is in prison. Those marriages that endure the time test can only be deemed as "special marriages." It is uncommon for prisoners to get married while they are in prison, but it does happen. Prison officials and most inmates alike, however, do not encourage getting married while incarcerated.

In this author's opinion, the Department of Corrections needs to implement guidelines to allow conjugal visits for married inmates. Conjugal visits have a beneficial impact on inmates, prison personnel, and society. First, they help to contribute to the marriage itself, thereby decreasing the chances of divorce. Second, for those inmates who marry while in prison, they offer a chance to experience and develop life skills that are advantageous toward the goal of rehabilitation. Third, they can be used as an incentive for the inmate's good behavior that could also be used as an effective management tool. Fourth, it would serve as a pressure valve for those inmates contemplating marriage, especially those who are experiencing the tensions of sexual frustration, thereby diminishing the likelihood for homosexual relations. Again, another effective management tool. Lastly, conjugal visits would restore a sense of moral brightness and fair treatment to a class of people who view this classic example of unusual punishment as an injustice. In other words, the Department of Corrections should correct this problem because it would be the right thing to do.

Endnote

1. In several SCIs, even softly hugging the spouse's arm and shoulder is prohibited. ✦

Part VI

Inmates and Staff

Chapter 14

The Unlisted-to Story

Why does it happen? Why is the pain of every day
translated so constantly into our dreams, in the ever-
repeated scene of the unlistened-to story?
—Primo Levi, *If This Is a Man* (1959)

"You talk and laugh with the guards as if they were your friends," the elderly, ebony-skinned lifer says to me. "But tell me, son, do you really think that these guards are your friends?"

I feel confident about my response, as I reply, "If they treat me with respect, then I give them that same respect in return." Since I was a child, my father had taught me this. Like everything else he taught me, I believed it to be true. Besides, I would rather have a guard like me than dislike me.

"You're a fool," he reacts without hesitation. "Listen to me. I've suffered inside these prison walls for the past 32 years of my life. I've seen everything that no man ever should live to see: young boys like you getting raped or f**ked, because they were someone else's b**ch back in the day when prisoners ran these prisons. You feel protected, because you think you can relate to these guards who are white just like you."

He laughs, then continues. "They don't give a f**k about you. Let me tell you something, young man. If a riot ever jumped off in here, that same guard you think you're okay with will be the same guard who has no problem beating you the f**k down with his blackjack. When you argue with them or disrespect them, you'll get the worse of the consequences. You're scum to them, a criminal, a convict who cannot be trusted. And when they cannot beat you down with their fists and blackjacks, they'll beat you down with their paper and pens (misconduct reports). You understand?"

I nod. Actually, I have always felt easier knowing that those who operate our prisons, including the guards, are white. When I have a problem, I can always count on them to help me, right? After all, they are still my people. This old dude sounds to me like he has an attitude problem.

"I was in this prison before you were born," the elderly lifer interrupts my thoughts. "There was a time when prisoners and guards did not talk or congregate with each other. Today, all these damn inmates want to do is talk, joke, and have fun with the guards. That's how they keep us complacent. We're nothing more than job security to these people. I'm not telling you that you should hate these people. It's okay to say 'Hello' and 'How are ya doing?' or to ask a question, but that's it! If you get too familiar with a guard, you'll start snitchin' for him. A majority of these guards are military veterans, racist to the bone, and have no respect for us. I'm a coonass nigger to them, and you're just 'white trash.' That's reality. That's how it is."

He laughs again. "A friend is someone you can confide in, who'll listen to your sorrows, help you in time of need, and share his sorrows with you. In all my 32 years of surviving this plantation life, not once has a guard or staff member lifted a finger to help me get my freedom back. You understand?"

I am beginning to. "How did you do 32 years?" I ask.

"The Lo's mercy, that's how. Of course, I had to learn how to read and write. I read every educational book I could get my hands on. I went to school, to vocational classes, and every mornin' when I awoke, I'd read my Bible."

"Young man, do whatever you can to help save your own life. And stop messin' with these guards. They are not your friends. One more thing . . . be even more careful with these other prisoners in here who live with you, for they're even more deceitful than the guards."

*   *   *

That was years ago. At the time, I really did not care. I would from time to time see this elderly lifer around. Some prisoners dismissed him as a "nut." Others told me that, despite his bitterness, he had a lot of knowledge. But like every young man who was just beginning to experience prison life, I just did not care.

Years later at another state prison, I heard through the prison grapevine that this elderly inmate had died of heart failure. I thought of him and the conversation that we had. Whether he was right or wrong, there was at least one kernel of truth that I eventually learned the hard way: trust between prisoners and their keepers will never exist—ever. His story was one that I wish I had "listened to." ✦

Chapter 15

Time to Play the Game

As a child, I used to play various games like hide 'n' seek, Monopoly, Twister, and the familiar Doctor. As I grew older, I began to play more serious games like football, soccer, and the occasional "quarters." Whether winning or losing, I always believed that the point of playing a game was to have fun.

In prison, however, there is a different kind of game, a sport in which a prisoner tries to get what he wants at the expense of another. It is simply called "the game," because there is always a winner (the conspirator) and a loser (the victim). The only fun in "the game" is for a prisoner to succeed in acquiring whatever he wants. The psychological thrill of winning this game is an intense sensation that fuels the desire to keep playing and to keep winning.

There are many types of games played inside our prisons. Most games involve a hustle for material gain or wealth, while others involve spite, violence, or sexual gratification. Material gains include acquiring prison money (cigarettes, food, clothing, etc.) among other things. Acts of spite may include snitching on another prisoner, setting another prisoner up for a misconduct report, or spreading rumors about another inmate to cause that person trouble. Violence may include robbery, assault, or fighting. As to sexual gratification, prisoners employ psychological schemes to satisfy their desires through acts of coercion, intimidation, blackmail, or promises to "take care of" their intended target.

Until the late 1980s, prisoners also played "the game" of raping other prisoners who were young, immature, and naive about prison life. However, violence to achieve sexual gratification is rare in Pennsylvania's prison system today. With the increase in the prisoner population and with society's tolerance of homosexuality,

93

prisoners can much more easily obtain sexual gratification without hostility or aggression.

In "the game," prisoners who prey upon younger and more unsuspecting victims are known as "booty bandits." Once the predator has succeeded in establishing a sexual relationship, the mutual arrangement is most often short-lived, because his desire to prey on the victim has been satisfied. Now, the victim is nothing more than a used rag doll, a punk unworthy of any dignity or respect.

Unlike other games, the prison game has no established rules or regulations and is premised on the concept of doing whatever one has to do to get what one wants, at any cost. Only one unwritten rule exists: No one can be trusted. This ultimately causes conflicts and divisions among prisoners.

"The game" is most often used as a device of manipulation and deceit by prisoners against other prisoners or by prisoners against prison officials. Staff members too play "the game" against inmates when it suits their needs, sometimes even against other staff members. Guards and administrators alike issue frivolous misconduct reports against prisoners who are deemed troublemakers. They may tell prisoners what one of them has been convicted of. Child molesters and rapists are favorite targets of staff members who want to make their incarceration a more difficult experience. They may spread rumors that a certain inmate is a snitch or may even give him a gift or special privileges just to deceive other prisoners into believing that an individual is snitching. They are notorious for allowing two prisoners whom they know to have a homosexual relationship to cell up with one another as a trade-off for their compliant behavior.

All in all, prison officials are the master manipulators of playing prisoners against prisoners. Their resources for facilitating this stratagem make it very difficult for prisoners to recognize and prevent it.

Prisoners who can recognize game-playing prisoners and staff members try to avoid any unnecessary association with them in order to avoid trouble. Some inmates who grew up in prison have been playing "the game" all their lives. For them, it is the only learned trait that they understand. Getting out of "the game" is very difficult for many prisoners, and the Department of Corrections does not provide any program or rehabilitative treatment to help them to deal with it.

It is possible to stop playing "the game" if one makes a decision to reform his way of thinking. However, our prisons continue to serve as major breeding grounds for all types of manipulation. After all, it is the prison that houses those persons who were unable to conform to society's laws in the first place. These prisoners live and exist together as outcasts. They learn from each other as well as victimize each other. When they are released back into society, they will most likely find themselves playing "the game" against unsuspecting members of the free world.

So tell me, you wanna play "the game"? ✦

Chapter 16

The Times They Are
a Changin'

When I was president of the Pennsylvania Lifers' Association at Rockview, I spent much of my idle time in the Activities trailer, conducting organizational business with our staff liaison. One particular evening, we had an Executive Board meeting and invited the board members of the Jaycees (Junior Chamber of Commerce) to join us. At their request, our agenda was how to propose a meeting with the administration, as well as such other organizational concerns as coordinating a softball game between our respective organizations.

During this, the conversation somehow turned to the topic of ice cream. The Jaycees had an ice cream stand in the yard where they sold frozen confections to the general population during the summer months. The institution's commissary did not sell ice cream, despite the fact that both organizations had asked the prison administration to authorize it. Finally, the conversation led to another concern: the young prisoners.

In the past two years, Rockview had received many younger, immature prisoners, who were increasing the tension level within the institution. Aggressive behavior, violence, and blatant disrespect were more prevalent now than when I had first come to Rockview in late 1999. Coupled with the fact that security had tightened up, many of the older, wiser prisoners felt that greater hardships were being unfairly placed on them. Instead of being rewarded for their compliant behavior, they were now forced to suffer the consequences because of those youths who were causing all the trouble.

"When we open the ice cream stand this weekend, watch and you'll see that all the young boys will be trying to hustle their con games for some ice cream," commented a Jaycee board member.

Our secretary laughed. "Oh yeah . . . it's gonna get worse. With all these young bucks coming in here, you best believe there is gonna be problems this summer."

"What do you mean by that?" I asked.

"Just what I said, Bof. You got all these young guys coming in here. They don't care about nobody but themselves. You watch what happens this summer. And the guards? Well, they're gonna have a hard time dealing with them. In the end, we'll all suffer."

"Well," I said, "we have got to step up, talk to these young bucks, and teach them the same way we were taught. We must assume our own leadership . . ."

"It's not like that anymore," interrupted the Jaycee board member. "You can talk all you want, they won't listen. I was mopping the floor of the housing unit just the other day when one of these young fellas threw a candy wrapper on the floor. I kindly asked him not to throw garbage on the floor. I explained to him that we prisoners are the ones who must live here, that we should keep our housing units clean. You know what he said to me? 'This ain't my f**kin' house, and I don't give a f**k about yo floor!' And if you hit any of these young dudes, they'll get their homies and wait to jump you. They don't care about how old you are or who you are. They just don't care!"

I remembered a time when I too was a young buck on my first arrival to SCI-Huntingdon. I, too, was hard-headed, wild, arrogant, and cocky. As time went along, it was the o'heads, the older prisoners, who took me aside and schooled me on how to conduct myself. I looked up to them for guidance and leadership. Now *I* was an o'head, but these new, incoming prisoners were not looking up to me or my peers.

The ongoing trend among prisoners, regardless of race and religion, has been the traditional division of two main groups: the o'heads and the young bucks. As each new generation enters the prison system, the young bucks serving numerous years make the transition to o'heads, while the newly imprisoned assume the role of young bucks. So the cycle repeats itself. The problem is that each new generation of prisoners is worse than the generation before it, an indication that they are a product of a worsening society.

* * *

The ice cream stand had opened. I sat on a nearby bench, watching as hundreds of prisoners gathered around the stand. There were two windows open for business with long lines of eager inmates, most of them young bucks. A guard stood nearby to keep any confrontation in check. Most of the o'heads waited along the fence until the lines went down, preferring to avoid trouble. The young bucks had succeeded in intimidating others by butting in line, usually by allowing a "homie" to take a position in the forward line. One older prisoner complained to the violators, to which a young buck replied, "Mind your f**king bizness!"

Two large metal barrels sat nearby, serving as trash receptacles. Although many prisoners disposed of their wrappers in the barrels, many others were throwing their trash onto the ground.

The ice cream stand was crowded throughout the afternoon and did very good business. After it had closed, I met with the Jaycee board member working the stand, the same one who had complained at the meeting. I told him what I had observed about the young bucks' disrespect for others.

"And. . .?" he asked rhetorically.

"And you were right."

* * *

The reason for the ice cream stand in the first place was that several of our community leaders had convinced the administrators that such a fundraiser would serve as an incentive to the general population. It was not supposed to be a security concern. But the reckless mentality of the young bucks had caused just that. This younger generation was becoming a new incentive for prison officials to increase the level of security, not only at Rockview, but at all institutions across the state.

Most of the prisoners who had helped initiate the limited privileges we had today were no longer here at Rockview. The younger prisoners who had replaced them did not realize nor appreciate the sacrifices and progress made by their predecessors, nor did they care to. They took for granted even such privileges as having an ice cream stand. ✦

Chapter 17

The Snitch

Everyone on the housing unit knew or suspected that Mr. Yellow was a snitch. It was very rare that any prisoner could maintain the same prison job for more than five years. Mr. Yellow had held the same job for over 12 years. He was very friendly with the guards and staff members, perhaps too friendly. Although other prisoners received shakedowns in their cells and misconduct reports for minor contraband possessions, Mr. Yellow always seemed to avoid them, even when a guard felt it was warranted.

"I had this lieutenant instruct me and another officer to confiscate any homemade furnishings in the prisoners' cells," a guard shared with me. "He told us to issue misconduct reports for every infraction. I confiscated two such furnishings from Mr. Yellow's cell, but when I went to the bubble, the unit manager and the sergeant told me not to issue a misconduct report. When I asked why, the unit manager just gave me a look as if he did not like my challenging his authority and said, 'Because I said so.' A few veteran guards later told me that Mr. Yellow was a prison snitch, and that unless he committed a serious violation of the rules, to just leave him alone."

There is an unwritten rule amongst prisoners that unless we are directly affected by something, we mind our own business. It is acceptable to say hello or ask the guards questions, but any lengthy conversations are definitely frowned upon. Socializing with guards is the same thing as talking to a cop; anyone who fraternizes with the police is a rat or a snitch. Prisoners labeled snitches are often subject to retaliation or harassment from other prisoners. Although snitches are still prone to assaults, it is less common today. Prior to the 1990s, snitches were often beaten or stabbed to death. Although still frowned upon by most prisoners, snitching happens in a more relaxed fashion now, especially now that prison officials have re-gained control over their institutions.

I met Mr. Yellow a few years ago, and although we were not friends, we had always been respectful to one another. Despite nu-merous warnings from other prisoners that he was a snitch, I had al-ways maintained that as long as the guy did not cause me any trou-ble, I did not care what he did to others. However, I did make a point to observe his interactions with other prisoners, as well as with the guards. I was not going to allow others to influence my opinion. I would judge Mr. Yellow on his own merits and not just because everyone labeled him a snitch.

One day, I witnessed an incident wherein Mr. Yellow told a guard in the bubble that two prisoners were tattooing in their cell. I was just a few feet away, but Mr. Yellow did not notice me.

Later that evening, I overheard a prisoner say that two inmates were placed in pre-hearing confinement and issued misconduct re-ports for tattooing. "Yeah, and I bet it was Mr. Orange," snickered another prisoner. "That's all these motherf**kers ever do in here is rat on one another."

Only I knew the identity of the real culprit, but I said nothing. I decided to do something that I had never done before: I would ask Mr. Yellow for an interview, confronting him about what I had ear-lier witnessed. When I approached him in his cell and laid it out, he immediately denied his involvement.

"I heard you tell the guard that those two guys were tattooing," I insisted. "You did it right in front of me." I tried to put him at ease. "I don't want to cause you any trouble. I just want you to explain to me why you've chosen this kind of life. Can we talk about it?"

He refused to be interviewed. A few days later, however, he ap-proached me on the range. He was willing to talk if I promised not to reveal his name to anyone. I agreed, and we arranged to meet that night during block-out activities. It was difficult to find a place at block-out where we could talk in private. I did not want to risk any-one overhearing our conversation or even seeing us talking to-gether. Sparrows and stool pigeons have different kinds of feathers. We found a table in a more secluded area in the rear of the housing unit.

"Nobody asked me to become a snitch," Mr. Yellow blurted out. "I voluntarily give information to the guards because I want to."

"Why?" I asked.

"I'm doing a lot of time. For me it's a trade-off. I give them good information from time to time and get special favors in return."

"What kind of favors?"

"Let's just say that I get to live my life a bit more comfortably, without having to worry about write-ups. Also, I f**k young boys. The staff members probably know this, but they don't say anything. When I ask to be celled up with someone, they probably know the reason, but they just turn their heads. I don't cause them any trouble, either. All I want to do is make life in here as easy as I can, so that when I come up for parole in a few years, I can get out of this hell hole."

"Aren't you afraid of getting caught? Or assaulted?"

"Nah, because I know who to snitch on and who not to. Most of the prisoners who come in here are afraid of their own shadow. They're not looking for more time. If they do something to me, that's exactly what they're going to get—more time. If I give information to the guard, I do it when nobody else's around. Most of the time, when these guys go to the hole, they don't even suspect me. It's gotten to the point where all I have to do is give a guard a signal, and he knows exactly what it means. There are only a few I do this with, though. Most guards don't even like speaking to me."

He continues, "The fact is, every prisoner thinks that someone is snitching on them about something. Paranoia is rampant. Most likely, covert snitches make up less than 10 percent of the entire prison population. The majority of the time, prisoners f**k up and go to the hole because they either did something wrong or they gave themselves away. I don't go to the guards and tell them about everything I see in here. I never rat on my friends. If I tell on you, it'll be because I either don't know you or I simply don't like you."

No matter what one may think of Mr. Yellow, he is being truthful. Paranoia over snitching creates strife and contention among prisoners. We learn not to trust one another and often fight amongst ourselves. Consequently, we are less of a security threat to guards and prison officials. I have actually seen guards tell other prisoners that somebody they do not like is a snitch. Once you acquire this kind of label, you will most likely never get rid of it. Even if you are transferred to another prison, someone will always recognize you and pass the word about you, whether it is true or not.

At one time, if an inmate did not like someone, a fight or a stabbing often ensued. The choice of weapons today are "words," in the form of gossip and rumors. They can be just as painful but never re-sult in more street time.[1] Words can be sharper than knives or shanks.[2]

Some prisoners have no qualms about telling a guard or staff member that another inmate is giving them a problem. I have seen it happen a million times. Once a rare occurrence, nowadays snitch-ing is the norm. Because more prisoners are willing to snitch on oth-ers, it serves as a deterrent for further victimization. In reality, snitching is a standard means to an end, tolerated by both inmates and prison officials because it creates a safer atmosphere.

I asked Mr. Yellow if the two prisoners he had snitched on were his enemies. He admitted that he knew neither of them.

"You could have prevented them from making parole," I sug-gested. "Doesn't that bother you?"

Mr. Yellow smiled. "No, it was their own fault."

"Why do you say that?"

"Because they let me know what they were doing."

Endnotes

1. When an inmate's behavior results in new criminal charges that are filed in criminal court rather than being handled with institutional disciplinary procedures, these are referred to as "street charges" which can result in "street time," i.e., an entirely new sentence, un-related to the inmate's existing sentence.
2. Prison term which refers to a sharp weapon (e.g., a homemade knife) usually made from a piece of metal. ✦

Chapter 18

Asleep in the Deep

Approaching the prison yard one afternoon, I scan the miles of razor wire coiling around the institution that confines me. Concrete rises to the left of me, stainless-steel fences to the right. The entire yard is double-fenced with razor wire—not once, but twice. Every 50 yards on the outside of the second fence is a guard's tower armed with such killing weapons as assault rifles and shotguns.

The yard is a place where prisoners are given the opportunity to escape from the confines of their cells. Yet as I look around, all I can see are stainless steel fencing and seemingly millions of miles of shiny razor wire—constant daily reminders of where I am and why I am here. In the distance, I can see the "farmhouse" where Pennsylvania kills its citizens who have been convicted of first-degree murder.[1] I can also see the highway that allows visitors to come and go. And I can see the majestic grandeur of the most beautiful mountain I have ever seen.

Hauntingly, inescapably, I confront myself with the same terrible questions every day: What have I done to myself, and when will this all come to an end?

I walk along the track. Other prisoners jog past me. A friend approaches from the opposite direction, nods his head, and smiles. Directly in front of me about 30 feet ahead, two prisoners walk hand in hand. As they pass a guard at his post, I watch the guard's eyes follow them then look away, as though he does not have a care in the world. When the couple turns at the bend of the track, I notice the two embrace in a kiss. I turn and walk the other way.

Many of the men around me are those who drown their sorrows with massive doses of psychotropic medications (Thorazine, Haldol, Cogentin, Mellaril, Prolixin, Xanax, Elavil, Sinequan, Valium, etc.). Unable to control their mental conditions, they are advised by both prison officials and psychiatric personnel that they need mind-altering drugs to stabilize the chemical imbalances in their brains. The prison system is all too willing to oblige anyone with a weakness for these drugs—as a control mechanism disguised as a management tool.

When I see them, shuffling around the yard like zombies, I know who they are. To inure themselves to the horrors of imprisonment, they inevitably become dependent on these drugs, until their human spirits are broken down in a mindless haze. Their minds ultimately become their own prisons. Each milligram of prescribed dosage becomes a razor-wire fence that coils around their brains like the slow, crushing grip of a python.

Other men in the yard, on the other hand, keep themselves in physically good shape. They lift weights in the iron pile or play basketball, soccer, football, handball, and softball. Sports can become a mind-altering drug as well, many of the players consumed by it. These men rarely frequent educational programs, the law library, or inmate organizations. In my view, only in self-educating endeavors can prisoners learn how to cut through the razor-wire fences in their minds and experience true freedom.

I see around me prisoners who at one time tasted freedom while on parole but for one reason or another ended up back in this place. When I ask them why, most of them blame their parole agent. To me, blame always seems like an excuse or a rationalization. Parole may have its difficulties, but I suspect that these men made a conscious decision to break the rules. And as with every decision, there is always a consequence.

In my opinion, most parole-eligible inmates never take the time in prison to prepare for reintegration into free society. Nor does the Pennsylvania Department of Corrections ever encourage or take the time to rehabilitate these men. Consequently, prisoners are released on parole with their uncorrected antisocial behavior intact. Ignorant of such important life skills as education, self-esteem, and good citizenship, they become victims of the cycle of incarceration.

I myself have other priorities—the foremost of which is to save my own life. Other lifers, who like myself experience daily reminders of our incarceration, yearn to save their lives as well. Most lifers avoid expressing their true feelings, hoping to be viewed by prison officials as conforming guinea pigs and good candidates for executive clemency. Many have become desensitized by the constant presence of these high fences and razor wire, as if they were steel bandages wrapped around their mummified bodies. Together, we exist as the living dead, hoping that those among us able to survive the horrors of these concentration camps will one day earn the chance for redemption, if not escape our rendezvous with the only parole agent that we may ever know: death.

I glance up toward the nearest guard tower. The guard inside is keeping a close eye on me. I walk alongside the fence, examining the razor-like pieces of metal attached to the tightly fastened coils designed to slice up the flesh of anyone who dares to attempt an escape. As I keep walking, the guard keeps watching. Perhaps, he thinks I am planning to do just that. I can only assume that he is more interested in my suspicious behavior than in the inmate behind me giving his lover a blowjob under the yard benches.

If I walk around the perimeter of the prison yard twice, then I will have walked one mile, going nowhere in particular. If I maintain a sound and healthy mind, however, then I will not have fallen asleep on hope. For hope to exist in the life of any prisoner, especially a lifer, one must always be aware of one's surroundings, constantly educating and challenging oneself to improve one's quality of life.

The yard guards blow their whistles, signaling the end of yard activities. As I walk amongst the crowd of prisoners returning to their housing units, I am aware that I am going from one undesirable place to another. No matter how hard I try to change my environment, I cannot escape the realities of this life. If I am not careful to strengthen and protect myself from the insanity that surrounds me, then I too may become desensitized, destitute of any hope I may have left. Asleep in the deep.

Endnote

1. Executions in Pennsylvania take place in a building that prisoners refer to as the "farmhouse," which is located on the Rockview grounds and visible from inside the prison. ✦

Part VII

Custody and Security

Chapter 19

Shakedown

Fifteen minutes after I arrive at work, a guard announces that all prisoners must return to their housing units. No reason is given for this surprise, which heightens the anxiety that I and other inmates begin to feel. Men murmur under their breath, a colorful array of prison epithets that cannot be translated here.

Back in the housing units I enter my cell and lock the door behind me. Within a few minutes, word spreads that the prison staff is shaking the block down. The first thing that comes to my mind is, *do I have any contraband?* There are a few loose razors on my desk that I use for cutting paper—I dump them into the toilet. I also throw away any empty bags used to store food items. Otherwise, my cell is ready for inspection.

Guards, white hats, counselors, and supervisors can be heard downstairs on the first tier. One inmate upstairs yells to another, "They makin' us striz-zip, dawg!" "Striz-zip" is adult-rated pig Latin for "strip." "Dawg" is slang for "my friend." Prisoners who want to convey a message not meant for guards' ears use their own language.

A long time will pass before the staff reaches my cell, so I decide to clean and tidy up the cell. I douse liquid cleanser on a handful of toilet paper and wipe the endlessly collecting dust. I wipe down my toilet, sink, medicine cabinet, and television set. Then I consider the clutter of paperwork on the top bunk. Since I have a single cell, I store most of my documents there. I straighten the papers to make them more presentable, then I clean the surface of the bunk.

In the process, I accidentally upset a peanut-butter jar that serves as my coffee cup. Coffee spills onto everything. I grab my roll of toilet paper and try to absorb the stains on my all-important documents. Half the jar has also splattered the bunk, across my blanket, through my bed sheets, and into the mattress. Grumbling to myself, I find an old washcloth, dampen it with the cleanser, and manage to mop up the mess, but not without leaving a noticeable stain. Now I will have more damned laundry to do.

Another 20 minutes creep by. Two housing unit counselors arrive to announce that they are going to shake down my cell. I place my hands through a small aperture in the bars of my cell, where I am handcuffed.

"Gee, you guys treat me as if I'm a criminal," I joke.

"Maybe that's because you are," replies a guard who I know. We share a quick laugh before my door is keyed open.

I step outside and undergo a pat-down to make sure I have no contraband on my person. Then they enter my cell for inspection. The counselors search all my personal belongings, showing enough consideration not to make a mess of my cell. They inspect the sink, toilet, cabinets, and two boxes of files I store under my bed. Ironically, the only things confiscated are the bottles of disinfectant and liquid cleanser I just used to clean my cell. These products are given to us twice a week by the housing unit staff who, I assume, do not want prisoners to stash them in their cells. The entire shakedown lasts about 10 to 15 minutes.

"All right, Mr. Paluch, you're clean," says the counselor. I return to my cell, the doors closed behind me, then I place my hands back through the cell aperture. My handcuffs are removed.

*   *   *

At SCI-Frackville, shakedowns are a more frustrating affair. Cells are trashed in such a disorderly fashion that prisoners feel as though they and their property have been personally assaulted. Here at SCI-Rockview, on the other hand, guards have been trained to search cells in a more respectable manner, for which I am very grateful. Had contraband been found in my possession, they would have issued me a misconduct report. That is their job, but at least here the shakedowns leave inmates with some modicum of respect.

During the shakedown, we remain locked in our cells, all movement restricted within the housing unit. Until it is completed, our meals are served to us in the cells. A guard passes a brown paper bag through my cell aperture. With it comes a paper cup of iced tea.

Lunch has been served: two slices of bologna and two slices of American cheese sealed in plastic wrapping, four slices of bread, a cheese Danish, a packet of mustard, an apple, and a set of plastic utensils. Not much of a meal, but it will sustain us if not give us more cause for complaint. ✦

Chapter 20

Misconduct

I have little to do this evening during block-out, so I amble to the front of the housing unit to peruse the "Call-Out" sheet for tomorrow. I know my name will not appear on the sheet, but I check to make certain and to walk off some idle time.

As I study the list, a prisoner enters the block from his work assignment in the dining hall. I watch him approach the bubble to ask the guard to open his cell. The guard refuses, informing him that the guards on the ranges are locking down.

"CO, I don't want to miss my shower," the prisoner begs.

Inmates who attend night school or are returning from work are given the opportunity to shower, so long as they make it to the shower room by 8:30 P.M. The clock inside the bubble reads 8:24 P.M.

"You're too late," replies the guard. "Everybody else had no trouble getting back to the block before we started locking down. You should have been here."

"But CO, I'm a kitchen worker," argues the prisoner. "We're allowed to take showers until 8:30 P.M. I need to take a shower."

The guard knows this to be true. For whatever reason, however, he will not allow this man access to his cell so he can get ready in the remaining six minutes. Although most staff members would understand the situation, this particular guard has a reputation for being troublesome.

"Listen, I told you before," he insists, "we're locking down right now. You should've been here by 8:15 P.M. like everyone else." Then he adds sarcastically, "See ya later."

The prisoner takes serious offense to this. Experience should have taught him by now that one trap an inmate must avoid is a confrontation with prison personnel. As he is a friend of mine, I am tempted to interfere and encourage him to walk away. But I choose wisely not to get involved. It is too late anyway, as I know this prisoner follows the common credo that backing down is a sign of weakness.

"Excuse me," he says, "you can tell me anything you want—but you don't have to talk to me like that. I ain't no kid!"

"See ya later," repeats the guard. He waves him away dismissively, which only provokes the prisoner further.

"Man, I asked you not to speak to me like that," he retorts angrily.

"That's it!" yells the guard. "Give me your ID card!"

The prisoner produces his ID card and hands it to the guard through the bubble window. A misconduct report seems to be forthcoming, even though the prisoner has technically not done anything wrong. I assume the guard will note some comments on his block card,[1] such as "Inmate challenges authority." The guard approaches the sergeant to make a complaint. I assume the entire scene has ended and walk away.

After evening lockdown and standing count, a lieutenant and three guards come to my friend's cell, handcuff him, and escort him to the administrative custody holding cells. There is no doubt in my mind that the bubble guard had the prisoner locked up in "pre-hearing confinement." I have seen this happen a thousand times, but I am nonetheless curious about the outcome.

*   *   *

The following day, I cross to the other side of the housing unit where the custody cells are located. A wall of screens separates the general population prisoners from those on AC status. I find my friend in a cell, sitting on a bunk, staring at a wall. As if by instinct, he registers my presence and comes to the bars.

"Got any smokes?" he asks.

I do not smoke, and prisoners on AC status are not permitted to have tobacco products. A sign on the partition of the screens warns that "prisoners passing contraband to AC status prisoners will be subject to a misconduct." I have no intention of joining my friend in the next cell. "Sorry. Can't help you."

He turns agitated, but not about the cigarette. "This f**kin' guard locked me up! He lied on me!"

"Calm down," I tell him. "What happened?" I do not mention that I witnessed his whole exchange with the bubble guard.

"I come back from working in the kitchen, I ask the CO to open my cell so I can go take my shower. He tells me no, then gets all loud with me, talkin' to me like I'm some kinda kid or somethin'. I tell him not to talk to me like that, so he asks for my ID card. The f**kin' guard wrote me up for 'threatening an employee or his family with bodily harm!' Dig this, I never threatened the dude!"

"You got any witnesses?" I ask.

"Nah, nobody else was around."

I know otherwise, but he is not the type of friend I would put myself on the line for. I do not need trouble from the same guard. Besides, no matter what I tell the Hearing Examiner as a witness, no matter how truthful I may be, it will not mean a damned thing. They will always believe a guard's version over a prisoner's. My friend is going to the RHU. I know it, and so does he.

* * *

Many prison guards issue frivolous or "spiced-up" misconduct reports, the ultimate weapon of choice when a prisoner challenges their authority or disrespects them. They may lie against an innocent inmate, simply because they do not like him for some reason. They rarely have to worry about getting caught, especially if no other staff members are present or aware that a misconduct report has been filed maliciously. Nor would any fellow guard try to correct the situation. A longstanding, unwritten rule between guards dictates that they never go against each other over a conflict between a staff member and a prisoner.

When a guard issues a misconduct report, the official procedure is that the shift commander reads the report, investigates whether it was warranted, then authorizes any pending action (such as referring the matter for informal resolution or placing the prisoner under pre-hearing confinement). Nearly every misconduct report implies that the shift commander has fully investigated the matter and approved the report. Everyone knows, however, that the shift commander conducts no such investigation and simply accepts the staff member's report as true.

A serious misconduct report, warranted or not, can be very damaging for a prisoner, especially if he is eligible for parole. Any time an inmate is found guilty of a "Class One" infraction (the most serious misconduct violation), any prerelease status in effect will be revoked, he may lose a favorable parole recommendation or be denied parole altogether, or he will lose a job assignment or any other program eligibility necessary to make parole. When drugs are involved, prisoners automatically lose their contact-visit status, each infraction sanctioning a period of six months. On the third infraction, contact visits are lost forever. If the prisoner is on "idle pay," he may lose his only source of money for an extended period of time.

For a lifer, misconduct reports have less significant meaning, unless of course he is a candidate for clemency or his dream of parole eligibility may someday be in sight. For many lifers, however, release from prison is a fantasy. Pennsylvania lifers tend to be the least troublesome of all state prisoners, though many younger lifers simply do not care about misconduct reports for the most serious of infractions.

*   *   *

My friend who wanted his shower never gets it. Instead, he will spend 60 days in the RHU. He will lose valuable school time to attain his GED, as well as his job assignment in the kitchen. He will lose time attending a "Stress and Anger Management" program. Ultimately, he will lose any chance of receiving parole—all because of a guard who couldn't care less.

Several weeks later, he is finally released from the RHU. "I feel like punching that guard right in the face," he tells me. I advise him against doing anything that will result in more serious problems, such as more time in the RHU, a possible transfer, loss of parole, or even facing more street charges.[2] But he does not care anymore, having already lost everything. I know that this is just his anger speaking. Still, I caution him to stay away from that guard and, if the situation arises again, just walk away and ask someone for help in filing a grievance.

He looks at me sadly and says, "Damn, my mother and my two sons were supposed to come visit me the week after this happened. I haven't seen them in three years." I understand what he is feeling but can say nothing to ease his pain.

*　　*　　*

Many years ago at SCI-Frackville, I was using the phone when a guard on the housing unit yelled at me, "Paluch, your time is up! If the DA didn't get all the information you've been providing, you'll have to give it to him later."

He thought his comments were funny, but I was not laughing—I was furious. Some prisoners within earshot may be smart enough to know he was joking around, but others might mistakenly assume that I was a snitch, a potentially harmful label. Hanging up the phone, I said nothing and returned to my cell. When meal lines were over, I approached the guard where no one could eavesdrop on us.

"Can I speak with you?" I asked him.

"I'm listening," he replied.

"You may or may not have realized it, but you disrespected me when you made those comments about me speaking to the district attorney. You implied that I was a snitch, and you may have caused me some trouble. I've always been respectful to you, and all I ask is that you extend the same courtesy to me, whether you like me or not."

I braced myself for trouble. But to my surprise, the guard admitted he was just joking and actually apologized for his remarks. In the days and months that followed, I was able to gain his respect. There were no more problems between us.

Prisoners have the power to walk away from problems if they are able to recognize them. Most trouble can be prevented simply by using creative and critical thinking. Unfortunately, many prisoners do not have these skills, nor are they taught how to acquire them, thus making it more difficult to avoid trouble.

A misconduct report is often a matter in which trouble is unavoidable. When such reports are issued falsely, inmates are totally powerless to defend themselves against the charges or a staff member's version. Although there are federal laws that provide a general guideline as to how misconduct hearings are conducted by prison officials, prisoners do not enjoy the same due process rights to defend themselves as one would have in a court of law. Whether legitimate or false, misconduct reports can deprive prisoners of parole, a form of cruel and unusual punishment by extending their time of imprisonment.

Endnotes

1. Pennsylvania prisons keep a file of index cards, called "block cards," that contain the name, number, and photo identification of prisoners confined to each housing unit. Guards normally use block cards to record minor infractions instead of issuing a misconduct report. However, if a prisoner's block card has one or more records of the same infractions, a guard may choose instead to issue a misconduct report.

2. When an inmate's behavior results in new criminal charges that are filed in criminal court rather than being handled with institutional disciplinary procedures, these are referred to as "street charges" which can result in "street time," i.e., an entirely new sentence, unrelated to the inmate's existing sentence. ✦

Chapter 21

The Setup

As a prisoner, many things can happen to you that are beyond your control. If you are not careful, you can work hard for years then suddenly lose everything you have achieved. The following is a true and accurate account of my experiences as the victim of a setup.

One lazy Sunday afternoon, I am strolling along the second tier of D-Block when I notice several prisoners gathered together in laughter. As I join them, one of them hands me a brown paper bag. Inside is a large phallus constructed from toilet paper. Written on the phallus in dark ink are the words *FAT ASS CORN*.

Officer Corn is a bothersome guard who seems to go out of his way to be disrespectful to prisoners, one of those types who issue misconduct reports for trivial reasons. I have to admit, the phallus is really funny.

I hand the bag down to the bottom tier to Mr. Pumpkin, an older, fellow lifer who is a bit of a jokester and prankster himself. "Holy sh**!" he exclaims, reacting to the phallus inside. "Do you want it back?"

"No, you can have it." Since the original bag holder is gone, I assume the phallus is meant to share with others for a good laugh. Then Mr. Pumpkin decides he does not want it. "Leave it on the table or something," I tell him, "just get rid of it." I go back toward my cell.

Shortly, Officer Corn himself comes walking down the bottom tier, closing cell doors. Instead of disposing of the bag, Mr. Pumpkin surrenders it to Officer Corn, who becomes furious.

After a brief interrogation, Mr. Pumpkin tells him, "The Jewboy gave it to me."

Officer Corn glares up at me outside my cell and shouts: "I'm gonna burn you!"

As he heads angrily back to the bubble, I yell back that I did not make the damned thing. My anger turns on Mr. Pumpkin for snitching on me, something which he finds somewhat amusing.

*   *   *

An afternoon bell rings, followed by the sergeant's voice over the loudspeaker: "Standing count. Be in your cell standing with your light on. Standing count."

My cell is a mess, so I decide to clean it up while waiting for the count to clear. There are dust bunnies under my bed, and I tell myself that I am glad that they do not have teeth. I wipe the floor down three times, just like I used to watch my mother do in the kitchen when I was younger.

Two guards walk by my cell, taking count, each holding a clipboard and a pen. I change my clothes and prepare to leave. When count finally clears, I proceed to the yard to play defense in the soccer game with my Hispanic friends. At half time, I normally take a break to have a shower. Today, however, my friends convince me to stay out and continue playing.

By 3:50 P.M., yard time is over. I hurry back to my cell in my soaking wet clothes to wash up before evening supper. I reach my cell and remove my lock, but the door will not open. Guards usually unlock all the doors electronically, but they apparently forgot to hit my cell.

Suddenly, two guards come toward me, one of them holding a metal box for a shakedown. A gut feeling tells me that my cell is the object of their search. I recognize the older guard as Officer Turnip, for whom I recently refinished a ranger belt in the Hobby Shop.

"Are you Paluch?" he asks me. I acknowledge that I am, and he asks for my ID card and tells me that the shift commander ordered an "investigative search" of my cell. The younger guard remains quiet and expressionless.

"Are you guys here because of Officer Corn?" I wonder aloud, suspecting that the guard who threatened to burn me has something to do with this surprise visit.

"I don't know anything about Corn," answers Officer Turnip. "The shift commander instructed us to search everything and 'leave no page unturned.'"

They enter my cell. The younger guard asks if I have any loose razors. I point out two razors on my desk, which I use to cut paper. The guard confiscates them with rubber gloves, a cautionary step against contamination, given prison's epidemic of blood diseases like hepatitis and HIV.

Officer Turnip immediately searches the top of my bunk, while his partner searches my desk. "You'd better take a seat outside the cell," he advises me. "This is going to be a while." I take my chair outside my door and sit down.

Officer Turnip then asks me, "Oh, did I ask you if you have any contraband in your cell?" I tell him that I have no contraband. Then he picks up something that looks like folded paper. "Does this belong to you?"

I look at the item and assume it might be a napkin used to bring sugar back from the dining hall, but it is too small and flat. "No, I've never seen it before." I ask him to open it up.

When he unfolds it, inside is what appears to be a small cellophane bag. Upon closer inspection, it seems to be a small amount of herbal substance that resembles oregano or marijuana.

"We're gonna have to get this tested," says Officer Turnip. "It looks like weed."

I am totally shocked, since I have never done any drugs in my entire life. When I left the cell at 2 P.M., I tell him, this bag was not on my bunk because I had just straightened it up. "Are you guys trying to set me up?"

He gives me a stern glance and replies, "I found it in this envelope." He picks up a small envelope that my father sent me with a letter and a cash receipt for a $20 money order used to pay for his reservation at the upcoming PLAR banquet.

"How did you find that in my father's letter?" At this point, my anger is rising.

Officer Turnip replies, "I didn't say I found it inside the envelope. I found it on top of the envelope or around it."

Convinced this is a setup, I have nothing further to say to them. I do not know the exact contents of the cellophane bag, but I have no doubt in my mind that it will test positive for marijuana. Within a half hour, they finish their search and leave my cell completely trashed.

*   *   *

Confused and upset, I have a million thoughts racing through my mind. In the dining hall, I show no interest in our semi-edible evening supper of thin slices of turkey-ham and bologna on stale bread with a bowl of vegetable soup. I return to my housing unit, anxious to speak with the shift commander, who is unavailable. Soon, I will have to deal with the mess inside my cell.

During block-out, I hasten to the unit manager's office to speak to the block lieutenant on duty. He is someone who I like and respect. Lighting his cigarette, he exhales a cloud of smoke, "I heard what happened."

"I'm being set up," I insist.

"I spoke with the shift commander. It tested positive for marijuana."

"Does this mean I'll be issued a misconduct report?"

He nods his head. My stomach tightens, as he continues. "There's nothing I can do. It was found in your cell, so a misconduct report must be issued. You know how these things work."

"I've never messed with drugs in my entire life. Someone is out to get me."

"I know. It looks too suspicious, and I told the shift commander someone may have thrown it in your cell. Have any idea of who might have done that?"

I relate the incident with Officer Corn, to which he balks: "I don't think Corn would go to such an extreme."

For a moment, I almost agree with him. But the fact is, guards have a long-standing history of setting prisoners up, so Officer Corn's possible involvement cannot be dismissed. His public threat to burn me already establishes a prima facie case with Corn as Suspect Number One.

"Does that mean I'll be getting locked up tonight?" I finally ask.

"I'm not sure. There's a good possibility you might." He inhales another drag from the cigarette. The tip flares a bright red, which is all my mind can see right now.

The lieutenant regrets that his hands are tied on the matter. He describes how he once intervened on behalf of an inmate issued a misconduct report over a loose razor, but he was told not to interfere with staff business.

"Paluch, you've never given me or my staff any problems. I believe you when you say the stuff is not yours, and that you're probably being set up. I wish there was more I could do to help you, but I can't."

I thank him for his counsel and leave his office, not feeling any better.

The main corridor is filled with the usual noise of block-out activities, but it cannot compete with the mayhem in my mind. I need some quiet time to myself, so I can think about what has happened, how it happened, and how I can prove my innocence.

Two inmate acquaintances who are watching television sense my distress. I tell them what happened in my cell.

"You were set up, Bof," insists a 26-year veteran lifer. "I told you these muthaf**kin' guards are vicious. Ain't no inmate gonna willfully give up no weed to set a dude up. He's either gonna sell the sh** or smoke it."

His companion, another old schooler, agrees. "Inmates don't wrap their weed in no cellophane. They put it in a plastic glove tip to keep it fresh."

"I told you," warns the first lifer, "if you kept fu**in' with this administration, they were gonna find a way to get rid of you."

I cannot necessarily discount this. Since I was president of the PLAR, I have indeed made waves for prison officials in a long series of political conflicts. As a result, I recently lobbied the PLAR's general membership not to invite staff members to our annual banquet as a message to the administration that lifers are tired of being neglected and their needs and concerns disregarded.

For a moment, I wonder if an administrator might be behind this setup, although it seems a bit extreme to plant marijuana in my cell. In most cases, the administration would simply transfer a troublemaker to another prison.

But a setup like this will land me in the RHU long enough to get me temporarily out of the way, as well as blemish my record. Perhaps the administration is saying to me, "Okay Paluch, if you don't want us to go to the annual banquet, then you won't be going either." I know that prison administrators have committed worse acts than this to hurt someone they do not like. So in my mind, an administration official is Suspect Number Two.

"Perhaps someone inside the PLAR did this," the second lifer speculates. "You know, there are some guys in here who don't like you. Some of these dudes are just as vicious as the guards and administrators."

"You know what I would do?" suggests the first lifer.

"What's that?" I ask.

"If these muthafu**ers were setting me up, I'd go to the Security Office and tell them, 'Yeah, the weed is mine.' Then when they ask where I got it from, I'd tell them, 'From the deputy superintendent.' Yeah, play them at their own game. That's what I'd do."

With an unamused look, I reply, "I don't think so."

* * *

As I return to my cell for the night, I realize that I am still not in pre-hearing confinement. My hopes are momentarily lifted. Closing my cell door for the next standing count, I am surprised by the arrival of the sergeant. He hands me a misconduct report, a witness form, an inmate statement form, and a receipt for the "confiscated item." The report reads as follows.

DC Number: BQ-3769
Name: Paluch, James
Institution: SCI-R
Incident Time: 1545
Incident Date: 6-24-01
Date of Report: 6-24-01
Quarters: D 2016
Place of Incident: D Bldg. Cell 2016
Misconduct Charges: Class I Cat. A #22 Possession or use of a dangerous or controlled substance. Cat. B #36 Possession of contraband non-prescribed drugs. #45 Failure to report the presence of contraband.
Staff Member's Version: On the above time and date while doing an investigative cell search, I, Officer Turnip, found a napkin that was folded up. Inside the napkin was a cellophane bag of a green leafy substance. Captain Cabbage tested the substance with test kit E lot control number 98011 and the sub-

stance tested positive for marijuana. See confiscated Items Receipt #A273424.

    Immediate Action Taken and Reason: NONE
    Pre-Hearing Confinement: NO
    Reporting Staff Member: R. Turnip
    Action Reviewed and Approved By: Capt. Cabbage
    Date and Time Inmate Given Copy: 6/24/01, 2100 hrs.
    Your Hearing May Be Scheduled Any Time After: 6/25/01, 2105 hrs.
    Misconduct Category: Class I

My nerves jangle, as I begin to experience the same tension and stress that I endured at SCI-Frackville. The inner peace that I had so longed to achieve in the past two years is gone. In the distant recesses of my mind, I hear the echo of my father's voice telling me to be careful not to lose my focus. Bitterness can overpower a prisoner, so that he becomes consumed by the injustices committed against him—he loses his ability to think and act in a rational manner. Right now, I have to coolly assess all the facts and circumstances of my anticipated downfall. Someone has made me a victim and has succeeded in harming me, but I do not know who. I must act as cautiously as possible to minimize the damage already caused.

* * *

The shift commander has decided not to place me in pre-hearing confinement, so I am able to talk with both staff and prisoners about how to handle this situation. That certainly is an advantage. But there is also a possible disadvantage. Prisoners found with drugs in their possession are almost always placed in pre-hearing confinement (administrative custody), pending the misconduct hearing. A few inmates may start to wonder why I am receiving preferential treatment and become suspicious of me.

I type a four-page letter to the superintendent, recounting the entire incident and asking for whatever assistance he can give me. Tomorrow morning, I will deliver it to the request slip box.

I am tired, but I cannot sleep. I am hungry, but I do not have the will to eat. In frustration, I throw the pile of boxes left on my bed after the shakedown onto the floor. I turn off my light, lie on my bunk, and try to empty my mind so I can sleep.

*   *   *

The following Monday morning, I go to breakfast but still have no appetite. I report to the Hobby Shop to finish making three Ranger belts for a lady staff member. I confide to my work supervisor what has happened. All he can do is wish me luck.

At noon, I procure a pass to go to the Security Office to speak with the lieutenant. I explained the events as they happened. But when I tell her about what Officer Corn had said earlier in the afternoon, she interrupts me. "Stop, I don't want to hear it."

"Why not?" I ask in confusion.

"If you're gonna try to put any suspicion on one of our officers, then we will not investigate it. Besides, the shift commander had to receive a tip in order to call for an investigative search."

"Where did the tip come from?"

"We don't know, because it wasn't revealed to us."

The tip had to have been made between 2 P.M. and 3:45 P.M., I reason to her. Whoever the tipper was, the Security Office should be asking this person how he knew there were drugs in my cell. Because it was an investigative search, the shift commander would have to know the source of the tip. Why not ask him?

The lieutenant promises they will try to find out the source of the tip, but she assures me she will not tell me who it is. No matter what I say or do, she adds, the hearing examiner will find me guilty. "You're not going to beat this misconduct."

*   *   *

That afternoon, I run into the shift commander, Captain Cabbage. Before I can plead my innocence, he tells me, "Relax, relax. We're going to talk to the hearing examiner and try to straighten this out." These words manage to calm down the anxiety and stress that have been plaguing me. But I wonder whether or not I can rely on him, as many staff members are masters at the game of manipulating and deceiving prisoners. A guard at SCI-Frackville once told me that white hats are given special training in this area.

After a shower, I approach my unit manager and relay the facts to him, asking him outright: "Do you believe me?" He has no reason not to believe me and intends to investigate the matter himself. When I leave his office, I wonder if I am hoping for too much. The hearing will be tomorrow. There is not much to hope for, but somehow I expect a miracle.

That night, I speak to a few friends in the yard about my predicament. They show their support and promise to do an investigation of their own. As I cross the yard, the eyes of prisoners playing chess and cards observe me curiously, as if they all know. Gossip and rumors always burn through a prison like a wildfire, unquenched by any presumption of innocence.

* * *

On Wednesday morning around 8:15 A.M., the bubble announces over the loudspeaker: "BQ-3769, Paluch, up front for hearing."

I have just finished brushing my teeth and washing my face. The night before, I packed all my personal belongings into brown paper bags. If I wind up going to the RHU, I want to make sure that my property is handled correctly. Guards often allow inmates (usually block workers) to pack a cell, which can lead to stolen items. During their property inventory, guards rarely care about a prisoner's personal items and will just throw them into a box. Legal documents can be torn or destroyed, and personal photos and mementos can be damaged.

I sit on the edge of the bottom bunk and say a prayer, fully acknowledging that whatever happens, it will be by His will. I close my door, lock it up, and head downstairs.

* * *

At the bubble, a guard frontally binds me with a pair of handcuffs. This is a normal procedure for two reasons. First, a prisoner may overreact to a hearing examiner's decision, and the restraints prevent a possible assault or at least keep aggressive behavior to a minimum. Second, if the prisoner is found guilty, he can be escorted to the RHU with little resistance.

As the handcuffs are locked into place, I glance up at the four ranges of tiers above and recognize a few familiar faces looking down upon me. Some of them, I know, hope that everything works out for the best, while others expect the worst. As the guard ushers me away, I hear someone call out: "Good luck, Bof!"

The humidity outside promises a hot day. I look up where the sparrows make their nests in building edifices, but not a single bird can be seen. We head toward the deputy warden (DW) building about a hundred feet away.

Inside the DW building, I am promptly pat-searched. One handcuff is taken off to allow the cuffs to be placed inside a belt ring fastened behind my back. I now have very limited movement with my hands and arms.

I wait on a wooden bench in the hallway. Presently, an inmate exits from the hearing examiner's room. As he passes by, he mutters aside to me, "Try not to interrupt the damn b**ch!"

"You're next," announces a guard. I am escorted into the last room in the hallway.

A large wood table stretches out in front of me. I am told to sit an old chair before it. The hearing examiner, a female whom I have never seen before, sits at the far end of the table. Nearby, an older woman staffer busies herself with paperwork. The hearing examiner takes a quick glance at me then begins to write something down.

"Do you have a written version?" she asks.

I acknowledge that I do and hand it to the guard, who passes it to her.

The examiner reads the charges and the reporting officer's version, then she asks me how I plead.

"Not guilty," I reply confidently.

"What's your version?"

I carefully recount the facts as they happened, but I purposely omit Officer Corn's threat prior to the incident. Nor do I mention Officer Turnip's suspicious behavior during my cell search. I have no concrete evidence to accuse anybody, and to suggest staff misconduct could provoke the hearing examiner to pronounce a more severe sanction. Prisoners are never afforded the same constitutional protections as ordinary citizens.

After I state the facts, I tell the examiner about my positive endeavors, such as my presidency of the PLAR, my job in the Hobby

Shop, my position as an HIV/AIDS Awareness Peer Educator, my writing of this book, and the fact that I have been misconduct free for over two years and have never been a drug user. Finally, I ask to call Officer Turnip as a witness so that I can question him as to his alleged discovery of marijuana in my cell.

This request is denied without explanation. The hearing examiner renders a quick judgment: "I find you guilty on all charges, because the marijuana was found in your cell. It probably was a setup, and if the Security Office wants to make a report to the Program Review Committee, then fine. You can appeal my decision, and if the PRC wants to reduce the sanction, that's up to them. Sixty days DC status effective immediately."

The hearing, during which I never once interrupted her, is over quickly. The guard hands me an appeal form, and I am escorted out to the main bubble where I sit with four other prisoners waiting to go to G-Block, the Restrictive Housing Unit.

A half hour later, a van arrives to transfer us. As we depart the DW building, I notice a lifer standing outside D-Block. He smiles at me, as the van passes by. I recognize him as an inmate known for snitching on prisoners at SCI-Graterford during a state police drug raid. I wonder why another human being who is forced to wear the same brown clothes as I do would find my situation so amusing.

Though angry and upset by this injustice, I rationalize to myself: I am going to a place where I will be given all the time in the world to think about what has happened, and how I will be able to recover. ✦

Chapter 22

The Restrictive Housing Unit (RHU)

The Restrictive Housing Unit (RHU) is a maximum-security facility designed to confine prisoners to their cells 24 hours a day. Inmates here are either sanctioned disciplinary custody status (D.C.) or placed on administrative custody status (A.C.). The majority of prisoners confined in the RHU are serving a specified amount of D.C. status, usually ranging anywhere from 30 days to 90 days per misconduct charge.

Both prisoners and prison officials traditionally refer to the RHU as "the hole," its inmates given a mandatory custody level of five—the highest form of custody supervision.[1] In the view of prisoners, the RHU is the bottom rung of the ladder. Although most RHUs are very similar, they are operated slightly differently in their specific regulations (e.g., showers, exercise areas, etc.).

Prisoners confined to the RHU are prohibited access to most of their personal property, including such electronic appliances as television sets, radios, and typewriters; phone calls, unless authorized for legal or emergency reasons; and contact visits. Commissary privileges are severely limited to a few cosmetics and stationery supplies.

*　*　*

The van transports us to a separate area of Rockview that contains a newly constructed building, the RHU. Upon arrival, I am escorted inside to a side room, where my handcuffs and restraining belt are removed.

"This is being video- and audiotaped," announces a lieutenant. "Turn around, face the camera, and say your name and number." I follow his instructions, speaking loudly and clearly.

"Okay, slowly take your clothes off and place them on the table next to you," instructs a nearby guard. (At SCI-Frackville, one guard usually performs the strip search, while another holds a baton to deal with any problem inmates.) I remove all my clothes, my boxer shorts last. A deep sense of humiliation pervades me, but I know that this is just a procedure. No matter how many times I experience it, however, I never stop feeling demeaned by it.

"How tall are you?" the lieutenant asks, probably to lower any mental barriers.

"Six foot, three inches," I answer.

"Open your mouth," directs the guard. "Let me see your tongue. Pull out your bottom lip. Top lip. Okay, stretch your arms towards me and let me see the tops of your hands. Turn them over. Good. Raise your arms over your head. Now run your fingers through your hair. Let me see behind your ears. Uh-huh. Okay, lift up your penis. Your balls. Now turn around and lift up your left foot. Wiggle your toes. Your right foot. Wiggle your toes. Now bend over. Spread your cheeks. Okay, get dressed."

My clothes are placed in a bag that will later be deposited with my personal property still on D-Block. I am given RHU-issued clothes that consist of three pairs of orange-colored undershirts, undershorts, and socks. I am then provided an orange jumpsuit to wear, a pair of white slippers, two orange towels, bed linens, an orange blanket, a roll of toilet paper, and a brown bag.

The bag contains two request slips, a property request form, a small tube of toothpaste, an unusually small plastic toothbrush, a ballpoint pen (placed inside a three-inch flexible plastic tube), and five institutional envelopes. With the property request form, I can acquire basic personal property items, limited to one bar of soap, one tube of toothpaste, one pocket comb, one washrag, one tube of shaving cream, a pair of shower shoes, one soap dish, a limited amount of legal materials, one writing tablet, and a Scriptural book.

The lieutenant asks a list of questions from a sheet of paper, such as: "Do you feel suicidal?" "Have you had a recent death in your family?" "Any changes in your legal status?" After he checks off the list, I am again handcuffed then escorted to a wing with a range of cells. I am placed in the first cell on the single-cell range. At one time, every RHU prisoner was confined to a single cell. Due to over-crowded conditions and the warehousing of more violent, problematic prisoners, officials are forced to double RHU inmates in one cell.

Inside the cell, the stench of feces and urine stings my senses. The lieutenant becomes upset and calls for inmate workers to clean the cell. Of course, all they do is flush the toilet, sweep up the floor, and quickly mop the concrete ground. Within two minutes, the large metal doors slide into place and secure me inside. The podhole (aperture) in the door is keyed open, and I place my hands outside where my handcuffs are removed. I ask the guard if I can be provided with cleaning supplies to sanitize my cell, but he tells me that the cells are only cleaned on Saturdays and Tuesdays. I will have to wait three more days.

Apparently, the previous cell occupant before me was transferred to another SCI. He has urinated on the wall and left his feces in the toilet as a going-away gift for the RHU guards. However, the guards are not the ones who will suffer because of it—I will.

Along my bed is a colony of brown ants feasting on what appears to be dried gravy. They are everywhere. I go to the sink, cup my hands with water, and promptly drown the ants. Using wet toilet paper, I manage to clean up the mess neglected by the inmate workers, but the entire cell remains filthy. After I put my linens on the bed mattress, I fill out the property request form.

My cell is approximately eight by 11 feet. The walls consist of large, white-painted cinder blocks that measure 15 from the floor to the ceiling. Above my cell door is a vent, and there is a smaller one built into the opposite side. Across from the door is a one-unit, stainless steel sink and toilet. The sink operates by pushing in a spring-loaded button, and a push button flushes the toilet. Three feet from the sink and toilet is a bed with an iron frame two-and-a-half-feet wide by seven feet long, bolted into the concrete floor. The bed itself stands a foot and a half from the floor. Above my bed is a wall light of two bulbs, one of which stays on 24 hours a day. At the end of my bed is a small steel desk with a swivel chair, also bolted into the floor. This doubles as a dining table and a writing desk.

*   *   *

There is a knock at my door. A man introduces himself as a psychologist and asks if I am doing okay. I politely tell him that I am doing fine.

"So, you don't have any thoughts of hurting yourself, do you?"

Somewhat annoyed by this question, I nevertheless understand that he is just doing his job. It is a procedure to have prison psychologists visit each new RHU arrival. "I have no thoughts of suicide," I assure him. "I've been down for 11 years. I don't like being in the hole, but it's no different from any other cell. Thanks for asking, though."

The psychologist nods his head, wishes me good day, and leaves.

An hour later, a guard opens my aperture to insert a tray of food. I transfer the tray to the metal desk then wait for the cup of juice that follows. Once I get that, the aperture slams shut with a loud echo that bounces off the four close walls.

A few prisoners in the hole know me. Although we cannot see each other, we exchange respectful greetings thorough the steel mesh windows on our doors. Shower time arrives, but I cannot go for lack of shower shoes, washrag, or soap. I finally find a hole in the wall where the ants have made their home, mixing a little toothpaste and toilet paper together to clog up the hole. This will only prove temporary until I can get soap, since ants are known for eating through the toothpaste.

After supper, I occupy my time with a few songs then turn off half the light and nap until the 9:00 P.M. standing count. Once the count is done, I again turn off the light, hide under the covers, and quickly fall asleep.

*   *   *

RHU meals are served three times a day in the same manner as in general population, except that the food is often served cold. In some institutions, RHU inmates are given smaller portions, and the guards substitute cake, pie, or cookie desserts with a piece of fruit. RHU prisoners who throw their food at others are sanctioned with a Behavior Modified Diet, usually consisting of scraps of leftovers combined and baked into an unappetizing loaf.

Outside recreation is given to RHU prisoners five days per week for one hour in length, usually in the morning. Prisoners must sign up to go to the yard with the guard making the morning count. Prisoners are strip-searched in their cells, handcuffed, then transferred to fenced cages similar to dog kennels, averaging seven by 20 feet in size. Once a prisoner is locked inside the cage, a guard removes his handcuffs. Some institutions only permit one prisoner per cage, while others allow two men to share a cage.

Most RHU prisoners utilize their outside recreation by socializing or exercising. Some cage up with another prisoner to fight, while others may revert to spitting or throwing feces at their enemy in the next cage. At the end of recreation time, inmates are again handcuffed, pat-searched, and led back to their cells, where they are again strip-searched without the handcuffs.

Showers normally occur three times per week. Prisoners are handcuffed then escorted to a shower stall for a period of no more than five minutes. This enforced five-minute rule begins once the inmate leaves the cell. While a prisoner is in the shower, a guard will usually search his cell for such contraband as unconsumed food items, extra toilet paper, and refuse.

Shaving privileges are permitted on shower days, RHU prisoners issued a disposable razor, plastic mirror, and shaving cream or Magic Shave. Nail clippers may also be issued. Prisoners are allowed to use these items for a 10- to 15-minute period, then they must be returned to the guards.

The one thing that RHU prisoners have a lot of is time. Few prisoners ever do their hole time in solitude, keeping to themselves. Communication is just as important as eating and keeping one's sanity. The RHU will make one either a stronger or a weaker person. RHU prisoners learn to adapt to their environment in order to survive the psychological strains that 24 hours of confinement per day have on a human being. Prisoners engage in a variety of activities to occupy their time:

    a) Sleeping: the number-one activity. Besides the usual eight hours of nighttime sleep, most prisoners adjust themselves to sleeping or resting during other times of the day. Since noise is much more magnified in the RHU than in general population, one's sleep cycle may vary, depending on how much noise one is able to tolerate.

b) Hygiene: washing one's body, brushing teeth, washing clothes in the sink (or for some prisoners, in the toilet), or cleaning the cell.

c) Exercise: calisthenics, walking, running in place, shadow boxing, and mattress boxing.

d) Reading and writing: library books, legal books, personal or legal letters, Bible studies, drawing, etc.

e) Games: chess, by far the most popular. Two prisoners construct separate chessboards using paper and pen, marking each square with a number (1–64), along with their own homemade pieces. Chess moves are conducted by calling out numbered squares between cells. Other homemade games are played, such as Battleship, Wheel of Fortune, trivia, etc. Some prisoners cover their toilet with a towel and use their sink for basketball practice, substituting a bundled pair of socks for the ball.

f) Socializing: another time consumer, talking to other prisoners. The most popular subjects of conversation are a person's roots and origins, women, and music. Arguments occur everyday, most of it harmless bickering. Inmates also sing or rap their favorite tunes.

g) Other common activities include daydreaming, fantasizing, masturbation, eating, window-gazing (if available), exercising, crying, and praying.

Suicide is a rare event, but it happens occasionally in both RHU and general population. Such variables as the length of one's sentence, conditions of confinement, mental health, and human tolerance level are all determining factors that can lead to contemplating suicide.

The most common method of suicide in the RHU is hanging. Since RHU prisoners do not have access to rope or shoestrings, linens are often torn into long strips to make a noose. These strips can be woven together to make it stronger. The "rope" is tied to a ventilation shaft or the top of a cell door. The prisoner then jumps off a nearby sink, desk, or bunk in an effort to break his neck. Often, the length of rope and noose is miscalculated, which results in slow, agonizing strangulation. Other forms of suicide in the RHU include jumping off a sink, desk, or bunk—headfirst into the concrete. Another way is by hoarding psychotropic medications and overdosing oneself into a cardiac arrest.

The majority of RHU prisoners have a bad attitude to begin with. Instead of accepting responsibility for their actions, they blame their suffering on others. However, prisoners generally receive misconduct reports for two main reasons: they violated a rule or policy, or they reacted to a guard inappropriately, thus exacerbating the problem at hand.

Most RHU prisoners just "do their time," so that they can return to the general population to be with their friends, enjoy watching television, and making phone calls. Those who spend their time in the RHU in idleness will nearly always one day return to the RHU. Those who utilize their time to improve themselves and their way of thinking, on the other hand, will have much greater success at staying out of the RHU.

Endnote

1. In Pennsylvania, custody levels are as follows: (1) Community Corrections (Pre-Release); (2) Minimum Security; (3) Medium Security; (4) Close Security; and (5) Maximum Security. ✦

Chapter 23

Isn't It Ironic?

I love that young lady Alanis Morissette, I think to myself, as her voice and the verses from her song "Ironic" softly fill my cell. It is a hot, scorching afternoon, and I have decided not to go to the yard. I do not pay for cable, so I watch little television. If I get fair reception, then I will tune in to the local TV station and listen to some music.

It's the good advice that you just didn't take . . .

Ignoring the irony of her words, I just lie on my bed with my eyes closed and imagine the beautiful Alanis and myself in love, clutched in a deep, slow kiss. Aside from the humid weather, the fantasy alone is making me sweat.

"Excuse me," a voice interrupts me.

I look toward the cell door and notice a tall, thin man in his mid-30s. "Yeah?" I reply reluctantly, barely tolerating the disturbance.

"I heard you talking to another prisoner in the yard the other day about parole and was wondering if you could answer a few questions."

Some prisoners automatically assume that if one talks about law or politics, one must be a jailhouse lawyer. I am an opinionated, often outspoken individual who speaks intelligently, so they frequently approach me for legal advice.

"I really don't know very much about parole matters." I am trying to be polite.

"Well, hear me out."

I am tired. I want to relax. His persistence forces me off my bunk. As I make a cup of coffee at the sink, he informs me that he is doing a four-to-10-year sentence for aggravated assault. He stabbed an associate with whom he had been in the drug business.

I finish making my coffee, wondering how I can drink something so hot in this weather. I take a sip, then leave it on the top bunk to cool down.

"Are you listening?" he asks.

"Uh-huh."

He explains that he acquired his GED in prison, completed the Drug and Alcohol program and a Stress and Anger Management program, had positive housing-unit and employment reports, and never received a misconduct report. He has completed his minimum sentence, receiving the institution's recommendation for parole, and was reviewed by the Pennsylvania Board of Probation and Parole two months ago.

"Last week, I get a green sheet [a response from the Parole Board] in the mail. They denied me parole and told me I'd be reevaluated in a year. I just don't understand."

"Did they give you a reason for the denial?" I ask.

"They said it was because of the violent nature of my crime. But damn, I did everything they wanted me to do in prison, and I was expecting to be released."

"Well, you're classified as a violent offender. Since about 1994, the federal government promised to give funding to those states that make parole-eligible prisoners do at least 80 to 85 percent of their maximum sentence."

"You mean [they] could make me do at least four more years before I make parole?" he asks angrily.

"It's possible. In Pennsylvania, parole is a privilege, not a right."

He sighs with disappointment. "Is there anything I can do?"

He could always appeal the decision, I explain, but I have no experience in handling such matters. I refer him to another prisoner with more experience on parole matters. He thanks me for my time and walks out.

Since the incentive to maintain good behavior no longer applies to them, a large percentage of these parole-eligible prisoners will use their idle time to vent their frustrations, which will only contribute to more chaos in the prison environment. Many of these prisoners will serve their maximum sentence then be released into society.

I sip another mouthful of coffee, turn off the television set, and lie back on my bed. Closing my eyes, I ponder a system that sentences individuals to a minimum and a maximum term. Why bother giving a minimum sentence, if it is not even going to be taken into consideration?

Now where was I? Oh yeah, Alanis . . .

Isn't it ironic? Don't you think? ✦

Part VIII

Violence

Chapter 24

Firebombed!

At about 1:15 P.M., I am standing by my cell door in SCI-Huntingdon, waiting for the bell to ring. As soon as the afternoon prisoner count clears, the doors open. I rush to the yard to reserve one of the better handball courts. Today's forecast is sunny with temperatures in the mid-50s.

Five minutes later, my handball partner shows up. Presently, prisoners begin to call for the winners from the sidelines, making the "in" and "out" calls. I am not a great handball player, but this afternoon, my partner and I continue to defeat our opponents in the doubles match. My partner is a tall, thin, dark-skinned prisoner who, as it turns out, used to live near my hometown and knew one of my brothers. We have been good friends through the years.

We have just beaten another team, when I notice prisoners in the yard looking toward the block. Dark smoke is pouring out of one of the buildings. Perhaps a kitchen fire, I assume to my partner.

"No," he replies, "it looks like the smoke is coming out of C- or F-Block. I hope it ain't no riot."

We turn our attention back to the handball court, until the yard loudspeaker announces: "BQ-3769—Paluch. Return to your housing unit. BQ-3769—Paluch. Return to your housing unit." Why are they calling me? I wonder. Maybe I have a visitor. However, I am not expecting one.

Going through the usual security check, I reach the hallway that leads back to the blocks. A white hat approaches me with another guard. He instructs the guard to take me to the RHU. "What did I do?" I ask in bewilderment. "Why am I being sent to the hole?" The guard has no idea.

At the RHU, I am locked inside the holding cage. Minutes later, the white hat transfers me to a meeting room where he can speak to me in private.

"Son, do you know your cell was on fire?" he asks.

"No," I reply, somewhat astonished.

"Do you smoke?"

"No, sir."

"Do you know how this fire could have started?"

I shake my head. He looks very uncomfortable, as though I am not providing the answers he is looking for. "Son, do you have any enemies?"

"Everyone here has at least some enemies," I reply, "but I don't know who they are."

"Well, have you had any problems with any of the other prisoners recently?"

I choose my words carefully, as I do not want any more trouble in my life. There is nobody in particular who I think could be responsible for starting this fire. For all I know, it could have been an electrical problem. So I lie and answer that I have not had any recent problems.

The white hat returns me to administrative custody pending an investigation, promising to get back to me.

Around 3:30 P.M., I receive a DC-141 "Other" report. It states:

> At approximately 2:20 P.M. on 4-15-95, cell 651 in C-Block was on fire. This cell is occupied by BQ-3769 Paluch, but inmate Paluch was not in the cell when the fire was discovered. It appears that this fire was an act of arson and, for the protection of BQ-3769 Paluch, it is recommended that he be placed on administrative custody in the RHU until an investigation of this incident can be completed.

*   *   *

The following week, I am seen by the Program Review Committee (PRC) and told that the state police have determined that the fire in my cell was indeed an act of arson. An investigation will continue a search for suspects, and I am to be confined on administrative custody status, pending a transfer.

Later, a state police officer visits me. He tells me that someone threw what appeared to be a shoe containing a flammable substance into my cell. The fire was so hot that the guards were not able to open my combination lock on the outside of the cell door with their key. The carbon monoxide level was so high that, had I been in the cell at the time, my death would have been inevitable. For me, this is a wake-up call.

Whether or not SCI-Huntingdon prison officials have any suspects for the firebombing, I will never know. In fact, I never do find out who did it, although I have my suspicions. I spend the next six months confined to administrative custody in the RHU before being transferred to SCI-Frackville. ✦

Chapter 25

This Is What We Do to Troublemakers

W hen I first come to SCI-Frackville in October of 1995, I am impressed by how clean the housing units and the cells seem to be. Little do I know at the time how truly filthy this prison actually is.

During the first three weeks, I have been complaining about the bitter cold in my cell at night. Winter has come early here in the Appalachian Mountains, and at night the temperature outside drops sharply. My cell window does not close all the way, so the cold night air causes a constant draft. Even worse, a ventilation blower constantly blasts freezing outside air directly into my cell. When I go to bed, I wear thermal long johns, my brown prison clothing, and two pair of brown socks, then I bury myself under two woolen blankets. But it is not enough to escape the frigid temperature.

The guards on the housing unit find my complaints amusing. I send a request slip to the unit manager, but he claims that there is nothing he can do: only the Maintenance Department can turn off the outside ventilation blowers and turn on the heat. They officially start the heat each year on November 15, another three weeks away.

Other inmates complain to me about cold nights in their cells, but they do not complain to the prison administration. I, on the other hand, send one request slip after another to the major, the Maintenance Department, and the superintendent. None of them respond.

Nothing happens to relieve our mass suffering, so I suggest to other prisoners that they file a formal grievance (DC-ADM 804). Not one prisoner, young or old, is willing to do this—too afraid of retaliation from prison officials. One elderly prisoner tells me, "I defecate blood all the time. It is hard enough for me to get these guards to give me a roll of toilet paper to clean myself with. But if I file a grievance, I may never see another toilet roll again."

I decide against a formal grievance at this time, since I realize it may get me into trouble I do not want. However, I and another inmate, Mr. Silver, decide to write a letter to the Pennsylvania Prison Society (PPS).[1] We originally plan to ask other inmates on the housing unit to cosign the letter, but any piece of paper with multiple signatures may be construed as a petition, which is a violation of prison rules. So, we decide that a simple letter signed by the two of us will suffice.

Before evening block-out, I type the letter to the PPS, informing them of the problem and requesting their assistance in this matter. I leave two spaces for my signature and Mr. Silver's, then I sign the letter.

*   *   *

At the commencement of block-out, I meet with Mr. Silver who reads the letter then places his signature next to mine. During this, I notice another inmate whisper to a guard. The guard immediately walks over to us.

"What've you got in your hand, Paluch?" he asks. That is none of his business, I tell him. "Well, why don't you give me what's in your hand," he demands. I reply that it does not belong to him. With that, the guard marches back to the bubble.

Within seconds, the sergeant emerges from the bubble with the guard, both of them heading in our direction. Mr. Silver urges me to rip the letter into little pieces, which I do. I quickly hand him half the pieces.

"Give me what you've got in your hand!" orders the sergeant. I refuse. "I'm giving you a direct order. Give me what's in your hand!"

"What's in my hand is of no concern to you," I insist.

Without hesitation, he orders me to my cell. I comply, but I keep a tight grip on the pieces of letter. Once I reach my cell, I intend to flush them down the toilet, hoping that Mr. Silver does the same with his half.

My cell door is opened electronically from the bubble, and I walk inside. Suddenly, someone grabs my arm from behind—my face and body pushed forward into the cement wall. With one arm against my back, the sergeant tries to pry open my hand, shouting, "Give me what's in your f**kin' hand!"

"You told me to go to my cell—that's exactly what I'm doing!" I shout back, keeping my grip clenched. Outside, all the other prisoners are watching us.

I feel a sharp pain in my arm, as the sergeant locks me in a "chicken wing."[2] There is so much pressure on my arm that I am afraid it is going to snap. I drop to one knee and spin around to push the sergeant away, releasing myself from his painful arm lock.

"Keep your f**kin' hands off of me, assh**e!" I bellow. "Stay back!"

Two more guards quickly rush in and restrain me without further incident. I am handcuffed, hustled off the wing, and shoved into the unit manager's office. Then I am ordered to sit and wait.

A few minutes later, another sergeant walks into the office. Without saying a word, he squats down and gives me direct eye-to-eye contact, looking me over and staring hard into my eyes, I assume to provoke me. However, I remain calm and say nothing. The sergeant then rises and leaves the office.

Subsequently, a tall white hat comes into the office and orders two guards to stand by. "We do not wish to be disturbed." He takes a quick look at me and asks my name.

"Paluch," I reply calmly.

He takes off his white hat. I notice he has only one silver bar on his shirt, indicating that he is a lieutenant. However, he is not wearing his name tag.

"Are you the inmate who has been complaining about the heat?" he asks.

"Yes, sir."

"So now you're going around asking other inmates to sign a petition complaining about the heat?"

"A petition?" Denying that, I tell him that I have only written a letter to the Pennsylvania Prison Society, asking for assistance to get the heat turned on.

"The Prison Society? You actually think the Prison Society is going to help you?" He pauses for a moment and looks at his underlings to share a good laugh. "Well, I don't know where you come from . . . where *did* you come from?"

"Huntingdon."

"Huntingdon? Well, I don't know what they let you get away with at Huntingdon," he shouts directly into my face, "but we do things differently here at Frackville!" I can feel his spittle on my face. "You don't make trouble here at Frackville, boy! And you don't put your f**kin' hands on the guards! This is what we do to troublemakers!"

He suddenly launches his left boot into my stomach. The kick knocks the wind out of me, my head propelled forward. As my face comes down, a fist punches me hard in the left eye. My glasses fly off my face, and I hear them hit the wall. The lieutenant then pushes my face down onto the floor and delivers multiple body blows. I can feel someone else joining in on the vicious jabs to my back and legs, but I see no one. The lieutenant unleashes a final kick to my face under the same left eye. Blood gushes profusely from my face onto the carpet. I plead to my assailants to stop beating me.

"Take this piece of sh** over to Medical," the lieutenant says. I am ordered to get up, but I cannot. My legs are too weak from the blows. Two guards literally drag me from the housing unit out into the cold, dark night and across the compound to the Medical Department. All this time, from my cell to the office to Medical, I still have the pieces of letter clutched deep in my hand.

*   *   *

Inside the Medical facility, a male nurse tends to me. "What happened to you?" he asks, as he cleans the blood off my face and treats the wound under my eye. Before I can answer, the lieutenant enters and blurts out, "He was restrained."

The nurse apparently knows that normal restraint does not inflict these kinds of injuries. He asks me, "Were you being restrained?"

Again, the lieutenant interrupts, "You're here to clean him up, not ask questions!"

The nurse administers a butterfly stitch over my wound then bandages it. He offers me a Motrin tablet, but the lieutenant tells him that I will not need one.

I am then dragged to a holding cell known as the "hard cell." Inside, I am shoved face first against a cold cement wall. As the guard takes off the handcuffs, he notices the small letter pieces in my grip. He asks me to open up my hand. Again I refuse, saying nothing.

The lieutenant walks over and gently whispers, "Open your hand, or you'll get another beating." I am too tired and weak to resist, so I open my hand. He takes away the torn pieces of the letter. The guard orders me to turn around and take off my clothes for a strip search. I can barely keep my footing, my whole body shaking. I manage to stand before them, naked and beaten, while they grin and mock me. Finally, they leave. The cell door closes, and I am alone.

Inside the cell is a cold metal bed with no mattress, a sink that does not work, and an open window that will not close because the crank has been removed. If I want to use the toilet, I have to ask the guard to turn it on. I ask him to close the window and give me a jump suit or a blanket, but he replies that he has strict orders not to give me anything at all.

An hour later, I am issued a misconduct report for assaulting the sergeant who tried to take the letter from me, and a second misconduct report for assaulting the lieutenant who ruthlessly attacked me in the office. I am too tired to deal with it, so I just huddle in a corner of the cell where the cinder blocks meet. It is extremely cold, and I am totally naked. As I start to fall asleep, I pray that I will never awaken.

* * *

In the morning, I am jolted by a loud banging on the door. A guard asks through the Plexiglas if I want breakfast. "Yes," I reply, and I sit myself up against the wall. My left eye is swollen shut, I have a very bad headache, and I am dizzy. The guard opens the pod hole and inserts a plastic tray of food. I crawl over and barely find the strength to remove it. I am not even sure what I am eating. When I finish, I return the tray and request to see a nurse. The guard takes the empty tray and closes the pod hole, mumbling something as he walks away.

Soon, a nurse comes to my cell. I tell her through the closed door that a lieutenant and a guard assaulted me, that I am naked and very cold, and that I need some aspirin. She asks the guard to open the pod hole so she can talk to me face to face. He complies. When she sees my face, she is startled.

"Who did this to you?"

I tell her what happened. She asks the officer to close the cell window and issue me a jumpsuit and a blanket. I also receive some aspirin for the pain in my face.

After breakfast, the dizziness starts to subside. I take the opportunity to look at the misconduct reports that have been issued against me. Both are complete fabrications. I will have to defend myself as best I can.

I write Mr. Silver's name on my witness list. Surely, he will provide his version of the facts and back up my claim about the cold cells. As I have only been at Frackville three weeks, I do not know any other prisoners who might testify for me, and no inmate witnessed the assault on me. However, I do recall the name of another prisoner who was present during the incident with the sergeant.

I am also allowed to write one staff member on my witness list. I list the name of a guard in the office where I was assaulted. Perhaps he will verify that it was the lieutenant who attacked me, not the other way around. The worse he can do is lie.

The nurse returns to give me a few more aspirin tablets. I ask her if she would please report the attack on me to the state police. "I can't do that," she says.

The next day, the prison physician and his assistant arrive to examine me. They take 15 Polaroid pictures of the various injuries and bruises on my body.

*   *   *

Monday morning comes quickly. I am escorted to a room to appear before the hearing examiner. I learn that my friend Mr. Silver has refused to attend. I tell the examiner exactly what happened with the sergeant, how he assaulted me by placing me in a chicken-wing hold. I admit that I pushed him away but only to defend myself. I do not hold much hope that the examiner will believe me.

As expected, she finds me guilty of assault and sanctions me to 60 days of disciplinary custody time in the RHU.

The other misconduct report concerns the fabricated assault on the lieutenant in the unit manager's office. This hearing is delayed until the afternoon, so that the guard whom I listed as a witness can attend. I do not expect this guard to tell the truth, and I am not disappointed.

He testifies to the hearing examiner that the lieutenant politely asked me some questions, when I stood up out of my chair and head-butted him in the chest. This was the reason I was restrained, hence the injuries I sustained. I look straight at the guard and demand the truth, but he just smiles at me and sticks to his story. I feel completely powerless in the face of these lies.

"Look at my face," I tell the examiner. "Does this look like I had been restrained?"

"Mr. Paluch," she replies, "I have known most of the guards that work here for a long time. I believe you caused these injuries to yourself while you were being properly restrained. There is no evidence to indicate otherwise. You are a very assaultive inmate. You must learn not to place your hands on prison staff. I find you guilty and sanction you to an additional 90 days disciplinary custody status in the RHU. Have a nice day."

*　*　*

After I am sent to the RHU, I am summoned before a lieutenant from the Security Office regarding the pieces of the letter to the PPS. The torn pieces from my hand fit together like a puzzle, and he informs me that Mr. Silver gave him the other pieces. At first, I do not believe him. All prison officials are certified manipulators, trained in the art of deception. But I can see for myself that he has most of the reassembled letter before him.

The security lieutenant argues that this letter is a petition by Department of Corrections definition, thus an infraction of the rules. "Mr. Paluch, according to your record, you're a pretty intelligent guy. You should know better than to place more than one signature on a document."

I admit that I should have known better, and that such a letter would be interpreted as a petition simply because of its contents: a legitimate complaint against the Department. "The unit manager, the Maintenance Department, the major, and the superintendent have all been contacted regarding my complaints about the cold air," I explain. "For three weeks, I have lived inside a refrigerator. I'm not a turtle or a snake—I am warmblooded. This prison was given every opportunity to correct the problem. I did not file a grievance. I decided to get some outside help. I had every right to make my complaint known, whether you like it or not."

"Why didn't you just give the sergeant your letter?"

"My letter? I thought you said it was a 'petition' "?

"Why didn't you give him the 'petition' "?

"You've got the 'letter' right in front of you. There's no language in there to suggest any demands were being made. I did not give the sergeant the letter, because my personal correspondence is of no business to any staff member, unless it presents a viable security concern. Nothing in that letter presents a threat to the security of this institution. Had I given the sergeant the 'letter,' he would have found a reason to lock me up out of retaliation. When he told me to go to my cell, I complied. It was he who put his hands on me when it was unwarranted. I was not violent or assaultive—he was. I merely protected myself by pushing him away."

"We do not retaliate against prisoners."

"I was punched in the eye, beaten, and kicked in the face, and you're gonna sit there and tell me that you do not retaliate against prisoners?"

"According to my staff, you brought those injuries on yourself."

His convincing manner is worthy of an Academy Award. I decide not to respond any further. He writes something down then looks back at me. "If you go back out into general population, will you cause us any more trouble?"

"With all due respect, sir," I reply, "I never caused any trouble. It was your staff that created the disturbance. Had that letter been mailed to the PPS, none of this would have happened."

"What about the lieutenant? Do you plan to seek revenge on him?"

"I plan to press charges of aggravated assault against this ass-h**e. I would like you to notify the state police about the crime that he committed against me."

"As far as I am concerned, the lieutenant never assaulted you. If you wish to contact the state police, you'll have to write them a letter." He seems frustrated by my last comments. He rises and orders the guards to take me back to my cell.

A few days later, I am issued yet another misconduct report—my third one for this incident—for "possession of a petition." The hearing examiner sanctions me an additional 30 days disciplinary custody status in the RHU.

* * *

After a week in the RHU, I am finally escorted in handcuffs and shackles to the Property Room where I am permitted to inventory my personal property from SCI-Huntingdon. It is in total disarray, despite the fact that at Huntingdon it was all packed neatly in boxes.

I write a letter to my father about the incident, then another letter to the PPS, explaining the entire scenario and requesting them to come to Frackville to take pictures of my injuries, so that they may contact the state police on my behalf.

The swelling in my left eye has subsided, but I continue to experience blurred vision. I am afraid that I might lose my sight in this eye. The left side of my face is black and blue with a tinge of yellow-brown. When I touch the skin under my eye, fluid bursts out and trickles down my cheek like falling tears.

A week later, I receive a letter from my father, who has contacted our family attorney. He asks me to write him directly with specific details. I do so. The attorney soon writes back: he has sent a letter to the superintendent, demanding a response to my allegations as well as a written apology for staff misconduct. As far as I know, the superintendent never replies.

Three months after the beating, I receive a letter from the PPS. It read as follows:

> We apologize for not being able to respond sooner. Be advised that we are aware of the allegations you have made against the prison officials at SCI-Frackville. Should you decide to pursue this matter with the authorities, be forewarned that it may result in your being transferred out of the prison.

In the view of this so-called advocacy group against the inhumane treatment of prisoners, my letter did not have enough face value to warrant an investigation.

And yet, had I in fact assaulted anyone, I would have been on the next bus to another state prison. Instead, I serve seven months in the RHU, upon which I am released back into the general population.

*   *   *

The RHU is designed to break the human spirit. I counter this by using my time to work on my legal case and read history books and encyclopedias. During Black History Month, I challenge myself to read several books on the life of Dr. Martin Luther King, Jr., a great civil rights leader who was labeled a "troublemaker." I go on to learn about other such troublemakers as Mohandas Gandhi and Henry David Thoreau. Instead of breaking my spirit, my seven months in the RHU make me even stronger.

After I return to the general population, I remain a target of harassment and retaliation by Frackville prison officials for the next four years. Their constant mistreatment of me and their abuse of authority sours me to the point that I become consumed by it and lose my focus. Every time that I believe an injustice is committed against me, I file one more formal grievance. I wage a personal war against SCI-Frackville and the Pennsylvania Department of Corrections, but I do not choose my battles wisely. Inevitably, I am transferred to SCI-Rockview, where I will be given an opportunity to make a fresh start.

Endnotes

1. Since 1829, this private nonprofit organization has been officially authorized by the Legislature of the Commonwealth of Pennsylvania to visit state prisons, monitor conditions within these prisons, and advocate for remedial action against unsafe or inhumane conditions.
2. A "chicken wing" is a common hold sometimes used in wrestling when a person's arm is twisted behind the back toward the shoulder blade. ✦

Chapter 26

Rumble in the Jungle

Welcome to the jungle,
It gets worse here every day,
Ya learn to live like an animal,
In the jungle where we play . . .
If you got a hunger for what you see,
You'll take it eventually,
You can have anything ya want,
But ya better not take it from me.
—Guns N' Roses, *Welcome to the Jungle*

For Mr. Green, these words come true on a cold night in January, 2001, at SCI-Rockview, when another inmate tries to rob him in his cell. Mr. Green is what is known in prison as a hustler's "banker." The hustler in this case is an unknown bookie who sells betting tickets on sporting events like football and basketball. Since the hustler is in the business of making money (e.g., cigarettes, food, etc.), he usually employs another inmate as a banker who is entrusted with holding his monetary supply. Mr. Green is the one who keeps the "money" that this bookie earns through his betting operations.

Such a job inside a prison can be dangerous. Yet for some lifers and long-term offenders, hustling and banking is a way of life. During long periods of incarceration, these prisoners lose their ties and contacts with the outside world. Prison jobs are an inadequate source of income for most inmates, who without financial support from family or friends turn to hustling to make extra money. Hustling may include the buying and selling of goods (clothes, food, drugs, etc.), legal services, typing services, sexual services, painting and drawing, gambling, and so on.

Hustling is a big part of the prison community appropriately referred to as "the jungle." Just like in a real jungle, you have to be careful of every move you make, because dangers lurk all around you. Hustling is a reality in every county, state, and federal prison in the United States, perhaps even around the world. Prison staff members engage in it as much as prisoners. Whether it is a guard smuggling in contraband, mailroom clerks stealing cash from inmates' mail, or prison administrators manipulating contract deals, hustling is a manifestation of our human nature. It can be motivated by greed, survival, or a hidden desire to get one over on an individual or on the system itself. In the prison jungle, it can become a deep pitfall.

*   *   *

> You know where you are?
> You're in the jungle, baby . . .
> You gonna die!

Mr. Green is a white male in his early 40s. He is six feet tall, medium build, and wears a ponytail and metal-frame glasses. I first became acquainted with Mr. Green while playing a backgammon game called "acey-ducey." My first impression was that he seems to be a nice guy. But as with any stranger in prison, I practice caution. For all I know, he could be just another con man looking for a victim.

After I beat him in acey-ducey a couple of times, he asks me if I want to gamble. This makes me even more wary of him. In prison, a gambling hustler lets you win a few games so you can gain your confidence. More times than not, you end up losing all your money. This hustle is used often on younger prisoners recently entering the institution or those whom the con man thinks are most vulnerable.

Gambling is against Department of Correction rules anyway, but I opt not to take up his offer for two reasons: I am on a strained budget, and I do not know Mr. Green well enough to gamble with him. If I win, how can I be sure that he will pay me? If I lose and am unable to pay him, how do I know that he will not become hostile and threaten me? In prison, when there is the slightest doubt about a fellow prisoner, it is better not to take a chance.

In time, Mr. Green and I develop a mutual respect, though we live separate lifestyles. He trusts me enough to reveal that he is a long-term offender serving a 10-to-20-year sentence. Convicted while on parole, he insists that he is innocent but never goes into details about his case. Incarcerated since 1988, he became a banker to earn extra income. He realizes that his job places him in a vulnerable, at-risk position that exposes him to thieves. In fact, he claims, at least a dozen robberies have been attempted on his cell in the past 10 years, although only once with success. Like many prisoners, Mr. Green is without an official job; even when employed, the pay is not enough to meet his needs.

In hustling ventures, prison officials will turn a blind eye as long as an inmate is not drawing attention to his activity. As a guard once confided to me, "I don't really care if a guy is hustling, as long as he has enough respect not to do it in front of me." Some guards do care enough to issue a misconduct report, but most regard minor hustling as a petty infraction. So long as it does not cause them any trouble, they will ignore it.

SCI-Rockview has two large housing units called "wings." Each wing has 250 cells that can hold a maximum of 450 inmates. There are five tiers on each wing, with each tier occupied by 50 cells. Normally, there are anywhere from five to seven guards responsible for maintaining security in each of these wings. A guard rarely performs his security rounds alone on the fourth or fifth tiers, which would compromise his safety. Except during a lock-down for standing count, guards on the wings are usually outnumbered by inmates 75 to 1 at any given time. In fact, it is impossible to maintain full security without having at least one guard patrol each tier at all times. The prison officials realize this, and so do the natives of the jungle.

Because of this lack of security on the wings, inmates are able to engage in such criminal activities as cell robberies, rape, and homosexuality. During such acts, they often have other inmates "stem" for them, i.e., serve as look-outs.

In today's prison environment, however, most inmates just want to do their time in peace without any disturbances or problems. Robberies and rapes are committed by very few inmates, perhaps 5 out of 450 on a wing. It would be easy for prison officials to implement new rules to keep inmates confined to their cells, but that would serve only to punish a large majority who causes no trouble at all. To restrict freedom of movement would only create more tension and hostility, ultimately resulting in far worse management problems.

* * *

The evening standing count starts at 6 P.M. each night. By around 6:30 P.M., the count clears and a P.A. voice makes routine announcements. For example, "Okay gentleman, count is clear. Mr. Carrot's class is cancelled. All outside activities as scheduled. Phone lists in the showers. Movie in five [minutes]. Block-out!"

A loud bell rings, and cell doors open. Men rush down the tiers to check tomorrow's Call-Out sheets, take showers, sign up for phone calls, attend outside activities like gym, play games at the tables (e.g., cards, chess, acey-ducey, etc.), or watch a movie on the block television. Some inmates choose to stay inside their cells, watch their own television sets, or try to sleep amidst the perpetual din. By 7:30 P.M., block-out ends and guards lock down the cells.

Mr. Green is just exiting the shower room, looking forward to relaxing in his cell for the evening. When he arrives on the third tier, there are no sign of guards or inmates, which is not unusual. He proceeds to Cell 311, removes the large combination lock from his door, opens it, and enters without locking it behind him. He turns on his television set, tuned to a public announcement station that plays soft music. Then he takes off his wet clothes and hangs them on a clothesline, dries himself off, and dons a clean pair of boxer shorts. Turning his back to the cell door, he gazes into the medicine cabinet mirror over his sink.

In the reflection, he notices someone quickly opening his door. Startled, he spins around—a masked intruder swings at him with a Master Lock in a cloth belt. Mr. Green veers away his head, and the heavy lock instead hits him in the shoulder. In the intensity of the moment, his first thought is: "I'm gonna f**k him up!"

He lunges at his attacker and pushes him out of the cell against the tier bars. As the intruder's head strikes the bars, he lets out a gasp. At this point, Mr. Green gets a look at the stocky intruder, whose face is hidden behind a mask made from a winter hat with eye cutouts. He takes a vengeful shot at the attacker's throat. The man ducks his head, and instead Mr. Green's blow penetrates his mouth. Wincing, he feels the inmate's teeth sink into his fist. Blood drips profusely from under the man's mask. Seeing that Mr. Green is barefoot, the intruder tries to stomp on his feet with heavy-duty work boots. Mr. Green immediately jumps back to assume a defensive stance.

At this point, the attacker retreats and flees down the tier. Mr. Green does not try to pursue him, since he is barefoot and clad only in boxer shorts. He quickly scans the tier to see if his attacker has any friends. A cell robber rarely acts alone, but in this case there seems to be no accomplices afoot.

Mr. Green returns to his cell and hastily dons sweat pants and sneakers. He paces back and forth from cell to tier, waiting for the intruder to come back with reinforcements to seek revenge or finish the job. But nothing more happens.

Around 8:30 P.M., as the CO makes his security rounds on the third tier, Mr. Green informs him of the attempted robbery attack.

*   *   *

The following morning, Mr. Green goes to breakfast as usual. Upon returning to the East Wing, he asks the desk sergeant if any inmate signed up for emergency dental, in case the intruder broke a tooth when he hit him in the mouth. Knowing the reason for his question, the sergeant shakes his head no and remarks, "A guy with a fat lip doesn't give me much to go on."

Mr. Green, not expecting much from the Security Office, relates his story to the block lieutenant and the housing unit manager. He also asks his cell neighbors if they saw anything. The only eyewitness is his next-door neighbor, who claims he glanced out and saw Mr. Green and another inmate up against the tier bars. He assumed they were playing around and went back to his own business. If there were any other witnesses, they mostly likely will not want to get involved out of concern for their own safety. Perhaps, nobody else saw anything at all. Perhaps, it is better that way.

Mr. Green is convinced that the would-be robber was after his banker's stash, as he had a lot of money in his cell yesterday. As if boasting about the incident, he tells me that even if his attacker was successful in knocking him out, the man would not have been able to find, let alone extract, the loot. That was locked in a metal floor cabinet with a heavy-duty latch and a combination lock. I regard Mr. Green's unconcerned manner curiously. He just smiles back, like a man who enjoys flirting with danger.

*   *   *

Because of this incident, and other cell robberies in the past three weeks, the East Wing's unit manager implements a new rule that eliminates free movement between the hours of 6:30 P.M. and 7:30 P.M. Rather than locking down at 7:30 P.M., the wing now begins its first lockdown at 6:50 P.M. The unit manager assumes that this will allow his housing-unit guards more control, but I am not particularly convinced of that. Although he may have restricted free movement, he still lacks preventive management measures to ensure that such incidents do not happen again.

When Mr. Green's incident occurred, there were only two guards assigned to patrol duty on the upper four ranges. Even with the new rule, those four tiers still have only two guards to watch them. Restricting movement between 6:30 P.M. and 7:30 P.M. only serves to punish all those inmates who do not abuse their privileges, just because one idiot did.

For the majority of us, this new rule is unfair. One inmate comments to me that it was the fault of the housing-unit guards for failing to ensure Mr. Green's safety. I agree. Like so many other prisoners in here, I feel more comfortable when my safety is not compromised. A criminal-minded convict, on the other hand, may think: The less guards there are, the better. But in fact, prisons incarcerate not only career criminals but a very large proportion of non-career criminals who made bad decisions at one point in their lives. These inmates simply want to do their time in peace, preferring to live in a safe prison environment. They want to pay the price for their actions and get on with their lives.

In private, I have asked many inmates their preference: to live in a prison where inmates constantly assault each other or a prison where security is maintained. The large majority of them chose the latter.

In my view, people convicted of crimes are not imprisoned so they can continue to commit crimes, but so their behavior can be corrected to the point where they can be released back into society. Prison officials who limit the number of guards in a housing unit compromise the security of everyone, which is counterproductive to a prison's primary goal of rehabilitation.

When I first came to Rockview in 1999, cell robberies were far more frequent. Not long after I arrived, a gang attacked two inmates and tried to steal packs of cigarettes from their cell. One of the victims hustled a tattoo business, and the attackers thought they had a lot of money in their possession. One was severely beaten and suffered facial injuries. In the end, some of the gang members were caught and later transferred.

This incident prompted other inmates to get together and solve this problem. One suggested that they retaliate against one of the gang members incognito to send a message to the others. The idea was nixed, because it would have only worsened the situation. The point, however, is that security was so compromised that prisoners felt they had to take matters into their own hands.

*　*　*

Mr. Green's act of reporting the attempted cell robbery to prison officials is considered "telling," a close relative to snitching. Prior to the 1990s, telling was totally frowned upon. The unwritten code amongst inmates was that if one told or snitched, then one would be dealt with. It was deemed such a serious violation of the inmate code that a teller could get hurt or possibly even killed.

Today, for the majority of Pennsylvania prisoners, snitching and telling are the norm. In fact, they are so frequent among inmates that prison officials now consider them effective management tools. Without snitches and tellers, as one staff member put it, "inmates would get away with 90 percent of illegal activities." Snitching and telling have become so common that some prisoners feel comfortable enough to do it in the presence of others. Yet, if you ask any inmate if he has ever snitched or told on someone, he will invariably deny it.

Many inmates regard Mr. Green's reporting of a crime to be acceptable. "I would've done the same thing," a fellow inmate tells me. Another, however, expresses dissatisfaction: "Because of Mr. Green telling the guards, we have to lock down at 6:50 P.M. instead of 7:30 P.M." In my view, Mr. Green had an absolute right to let officials know what happened to him. Because of their failure to adequately protect him, he could have been seriously hurt or even killed.

"What was I suppose to do?" Mr. Green asks me rhetorically.

"The right thing," was my simple answer. In a prison setting, though, that is not always the easiest thing to do. ✦

Chapter 27

The Lock in the Sock

Watch what you say and do not mock,
For it may be a fist, a shank, or a lock in a sock.
Be careful what you do and do not feed,
It may result in a wound that is yours to bleed.
Mind your own business and do not cause strife,
In the end you may save your very own life.
Heed this warning so it doesn't cause shock,
For it may be a fist, a shank, or a lock in a sock!

Another dog-eat-dog day at SCI-Huntingdon, I think to myself as I wake up to the deafening ring of the 8:15 A.M. bell. The morning meal lines are returning to the housing units, and inmates are waiting for work lines to be called. Outside my cell, I hear a prisoner on my tier yell down to an inmate friend below. I recognize the voice of Mr. Apple, my next-door neighbor and a fellow lifer.

Mr. Apple is in his early 40s and has "been down" since he was 17 years old. Like many of the o'heads, he is part of the old school who grew up inside Pennsylvania's prisons from the 1960s through the early 1980s, a time when a prisoner had to literally fight for his survival.

I open my cell door and walk out onto the tier, when I observe a younger inmate step out of his cell in agitation. He tells Mr. Apple that his yelling woke him up. Mr. Apple turns apologetically and replies, "My fault."

As he turns away, the young inmate blurts out, "If you wake me up again, there's gonna be something!"

Mr. Apple stops and turns around. "What did you say?" he asks, as if perhaps he and everyone who was watching them may have misunderstood the young inmate's words.

"You heard me. Wake me up again, and see what happens."

Without arguing, Mr. Apple disappears into his cell.

Five minutes later, work lines are called. Around 8:30 A.M., the doors open for all prisoners to go to the morning yard. I play a few games of handball, until the loudspeaker announces that yard is over, then I walk back to the block.

As I enter the corridor to the housing unit, I see Mr. Apple in handcuffs, escorted by two guards and a white hat to the RHU. Back on my tier, the news spreads that Mr. Apple attacked the younger inmate who threatened him. He stuffed one sock inside a second sock then filled it with a large, heavy lock. While the young inmate reclined in bed, Mr. Apple ran into his cell and swung hard, taking a nice-sized chunk of flesh out of the youth's head.

I walk over to the younger inmate's empty cell. It is in disarray, and blood has soaked the bed sheets and splattered the floor. A guard arrives to board up the cell, pending an investigation. Another guard walks around the tier, asking prisoners if they saw anything. There are no witnesses to speak of.

"What about you, Paluch?" he asks me. "Did you see anything?"

Irritated by the question, and fairly new to the prison, I answer arrogantly, "I just came back from the yard. But if I did see anything, I wouldn't tell you!"

The guard seems unbothered by my words and continues along the tier, peering into prisoners' cells and asking for information. The fact that Mr. Apple is already locked up in the RHU suggests to me that either the young inmate himself told who assaulted him or another inmate witnessed it and snitched to the guards.

That evening during supper, some prisoners at my table mention that the younger inmate suffered multiple fractures to his face and head, resulting in twelve stitches. He was subsequently placed in administrative custody status for his own protection.

A few days later, I learn that Mr. Apple has been found guilty of assault by the hearing examiner and placed in disciplinary custody status for 90 days. Both prisoners are eventually transferred to other prisons. I have no idea whether Mr. Apple was ever given a street charge, i.e., charged in criminal court. Since he is a lifer, he could be charged with "assault by a lifer," which ironically warrants a penalty in Pennsylvania that carries another life sentence.

The moral of this story is that prisoners must be very careful about what they say to other prisoners. The younger inmate, by his own ignorance, made a bad decision to threaten another inmate who he did not know. He would have been better off to simply accept Mr. Apple's apology, because the issue was too small to be worth a confrontation. His error in judgment resulted in a violent consequence, one that could have cost him his life.

Given the nature of prison society, it is very difficult to walk away from another prisoner's threat against you. The offended party is under overwhelming pressure by his peers to correct such a violation by violence or some show of strength. If it is not corrected, the recipient of a threat will be viewed as weak and can be labeled a "b**ch" or a "punk." He is then vulnerable to further threats from other prisoners. The one who makes the threat, on the other hand, is looked upon as someone who has "taken the other person's heart" by establishing his dominance or manhood over him.

One cannot ignore even the idlest of threats. Some try to prevent these situations by making themselves aware beforehand of a problematic prisoner or prison guard and do their best to avoid contact with that person. However, circumstances arise when it cannot be avoided. Without disciplined self-restraint or critical intervention, these situations often escalate into a wrong decision, such as Mr. Apple's violent retaliation.

It should also be noted that when the prison environment is harsh and stressful, it can itself contribute to the escalation of these kinds of incidents. Most prison officials deal with problem prisoners by issuing unwarranted or fabricated misconduct reports as retribution, rather than providing them with counseling or treatment. This only increases the bitterness of such prisoners.

Furthermore, the Pennsylvania Department of Corrections and the Pennsylvania Board of Probation and Parole have made it more and more difficult for prisoners to earn parole through good behavior. This only exacerbates the animosity and hostility ever present in our correctional institutions. The absence of meaningful privileges and opportunities for self-improvement, coupled with the constant imposition of new rules and regulations, make it even harder for prisoners to do their time in a peaceful, constructive way. It interferes with both the ability of prisoners to effectively rehabilitate themselves and of prison officials to effectively manage their prison. ✦

Part IX

Lifers

Chapter 28

A Bowl of Fruit

Lifers are my people. I say this because the reality of my incarceration has made me realize that lifers are like a second family to me. In addition to being one of 41,000 Pennsylvania prisoners, I am also one of the state's nearly 4,100 lifers—all stranded on a slowly sinking ship. We may have come on board alone, but we are all on this ship together. If we fail to realize this inevitable fact, we will ultimately hurt our chances to get off the ship alive.

As lifers, we share a common bond unlike any other prisoners. Although you will rarely hear a lifer call a prison his home, we collectively understand that due to the length of our sentences, this institution is literally Home. When things go wrong inside these state prisons, it is the lifers who speak up. Even with the present restrictions unfairly imposed on lifers, we remain steadfast in our attempts to resolve existing problems between prison officials and inmates.

To put it simply, lifers are the stabilizing force for prison management and for creating a more livable atmosphere inside Pennsylvania's prisons. As one unit manager once told me, "If I had to choose between managing a housing unit full of lifers and a housing unit of parole-eligible inmates, I would choose the lifers." Why? Lifers are a more behaved group of inmates who realize that they may never live to see their freedom. Since this may be our home forever, we are the ones who want to make certain that the conditions of our confinement are less stressful and more pleasant for inmates and staff alike.

We lifers are like a close-knit fraternity, a solid unit of incarcerated citizens who hope that by our own merits we can earn a second chance to live freely in society once again. In that hope, we make strenuous efforts to obtain the right to parole consideration for lifers.

There was once a rumor that prison officials were considering taking away our existing lifer organizations. As a young lifer, I was one of those very concerned about this. One day in the yard, at an informal gathering of the officers of the Pennsylvania Lifers' Association at Huntingdon, I vented my concerns to the group. The president looked at me with a kindly laugh, his words teaching me a valuable lesson: "They can take away all our lifer organizations, but we lifers will always be an organization." In that and many respects, lifers are my people.

I would certainly not argue that every lifer in Pennsylvania is a model inmate, but a large majority of us are indeed examples that other prisoners would do well to follow. There are some of us, of course, who simply do not care to correct their antisocial behavior or are too criminally minded to bring about any change in their lives. As "family members," all we can do is encourage them to educate themselves. Advice and counseling are effective methods, but ultimately every individual lifer must be willing to make a difference in his own life. Many lifers who regard their situation as hopeless feel that there is no need to improve their way of life. When such incentives as executive clemency and parole are no longer a viable option for them, they continue their antisocial behavior for years to come.

For the vast majority of lifers who educate themselves and use their time constructively and responsibly, however, the element of hope is instilled by their need to excel in good citizenship. Like any other human being in this world, a lifer possesses good and bad qualities. From my long personal experiences and interactions with lifers, my conclusion is that they want what is best not only for themselves as individuals but for society at large.

*   *   *

Let's take a walk inside one of the 26 correctional institutions that exist in Pennsylvania. This could be any prison. Let me introduce you to some lifers who comprise only 10 percent of the total statewide prison population. Most of them I know, a few I do not. Whether friend or stranger, all of them are my family.

As we walk past cells in a typical housing unit, you can see the large slabs of concrete under our feet, many of them cracked. They are connected to the floors of the cells where my family members dwell.

We stop at a cell with a heavy, iron-framed door. Inside, Mr. Banana, an elderly man who has been down nearly 20 years, sits on his bed watching television. He returns my greeting. We briefly discuss politics, his favorite topic. Mr. Banana is not an active member of the lifers' organization, but he supports the cause. I ask him why he will not join the organization.

"Too tired," he says. "I was involved for over 10 years. We have made small, significant changes, but not the kind I had hoped for." He is referring to the parole-for-lifers movement. Many of the older lifers share his sentiment. I wish him a good day then move on.

Our next visit is with Mr. Cherry and Mr. Grape, who are cellies. Mr. Cherry, in his mid-30s, has been here for 15 years. His cellmate, Mr. Grape, is a fairly new lifer who has been down for two years.

Mr. Cherry, known as a legal beagle, is presently working on his own case. When I need advice on a certain matter, I know I can come to him and rely on his sage wisdom. He works in the Correctional Industries Shop. He is also a member of the lifers' organization, even though his participation is somewhat limited.

Mr. Grape, on the other hand, is a wild child who frequently finds himself in confrontations with other inmates and guards. He is not an active member of the organization, being, at the moment, more interested in playing basketball with his friends than going to the law library. He is young and immature. With proper guidance, Mr. Grape may one day come around and begin to understand the reality of his sentence, hopefully soon and not 10 years from now.

Next door is another family member, Mr. Pear. Celled up with a nonlifer, he is a peaceful Christian who reads the Holy Scriptures and attends Bible study with his spiritual brothers. I remember one day seeing Mr. Pear in church, singing a worship song in an unforgettably beautiful voice. His faith has convinced him that his Creator will one day deliver him from his bondage. Mr. Pear supports the lifers, but I have never see him at any of the meetings.

Farther down the range is Mr. Orange, a single celler presently classified as a "3YZ." The "3" refers to his custody level as medium security, the "Y" means that he is a lifer, and the "Z" indicates that he is a single celler prohibited from having a cellmate. Mr. Orange has been down for 18 years.

At age 17, when he first came to prison, he was angry at the world. "I didn't care about anybody or about myself," he once told me. "I was constantly in the hole for assaulting inmates and guards. Couple times, I tried suicide, hence the single cell." He pauses to laugh. "Ain't got no misconduct in three years, brother! Three years!"

Mr. Orange is a decent, personable man, but he is not a part of the lifers' "stabilizing force." He will not join the organization because he does not believe that he is smart enough to get involved. "That's for you educated dudes," he tells me. "I'll support ya'll if need be, but I ain't interested."

It would be easy for me to feel sorry for Mr. Orange, but I do not. I have encouraged him to go to school, but he refuses. Like many prisoners, he lacks the education to do his own legal research. He has stayed out of trouble for the past three years, but he is far away from ever winning his freedom.

We visit a different tier on another level. As we climb the steel-grated stairs, its iron railings are cold to the touch. The cracks in the foundation walls make me wonder when the concrete will give in and crumble to the ground. We reach the top step and turn toward the range.

Everybody knows the occupant of the first cell: Mr. Kiwi, who has served nearly 35 years for murder and has dwelled in this same cell for 12 of those years. What makes Mr. Kiwi so unique is that he began doing his time at the old Eastern State Penitentiary[1] that has since been condemned and converted into a museum. Mr. Kiwi always has a whole history of stories about how the system has changed throughout the years. He remembers when a certain superintendent was once a guard, and how numerous prison officials who began their careers when he was a young man are now retired. He works on the plumbing crew and has a bachelor's degree in business management, having long ago taken advantage of going to college when Pell Grants were offered to lifers. Mr. Kiwi is not in his cell at this moment.

A few cells down resides Mr. Nectarine, who is celled up with a nonlifer, his young homosexual lover. Although we know each other, we do not socialize. Mr. Nectarine is known to be dangerous and has assaulted many of the young boys who chose to live with him. He has no interest in the lifers' organization or our pursuit of parole consideration. Prison is his life. Since he cannot have a woman, he accepts what he calls "the next best substitute for a b**ch," a boy. I do not bother to stop at his cell and keep going.

Our next stop is another single celler, Mr. Raspberry, who likes to lift weights when he is not working in the library. He practices Islam and has an associate degree in business management. He attends lifers' organization meetings when he can. Mr. Raspberry is sitting and writing as I look in.

"Hello, Bof," he greets me. "What's going on?"

"Nothing much," I reply. "Just dropping by to say hello. Are you busy?"

"Yeah, I'm helping somebody with their legal work. You know, another inmate who was doing legal work for him screwed up his case real bad. I'm going to try to get him his appellate rights back."

How many times have I heard this before? "Well, I just stopped by to see how you were doing. I'll talk to you later."

As I continue down the range, I see Mr. Lemon entering his cell. He just came back from work in the Activities Department. A highly educated man, he is well respected among the inmates and one of the hardest working soldiers in our lifers' organization.

"What's going on, kid?" he asks, as I approach him.

"Just roaming around, I guess." I notice his plastic washtub with laundry soaking in it. "I see you've got some laundry to do, huh?"

"Yep. After years in this place and doing my own laundry, I'm beginning to feel like the Maytag man." He looks tired. Although I would love to chat with him, I respect his need for personal time and privacy, so I say goodbye.

At the end of the range lives the all-too-familiar Mr. Pineapple. His cell door is open, and he is loitering on the range, talking to a neighbor. He works in the Laundry Department, but he earns his keep as a hustler. For two packs of cigarettes a month, he will take your dirty laundry to his work detail and have your clothes washed and pressed. If you need a little bleach for your whites, he is your man. He also runs a food store on the block. "If you've got a pack, I've got the snack," he likes to say. If you do not have a pack, he will offer you a two-for-one deal until payroll week. If you borrow a bag of potato chips, you will have to pay him two bags in return.

Mr. Pineapple gives me business as well, at times hiring me to edit or type a few letters for him. When I am hungry, I know Mr.

Pineapple will kindly give me a bag of potato chips or whatever I may need, in exchange for equal services. In other words, I can get a one-for-one deal on the barter system.

I glance inside his cell at the wall near the door, half of it covered with photographs of family and friends, the other half with beautiful naked women.

"What's going on with you?" he asks.

"Not too much," I reply. "Rumor has it you're going to join the organization?"

He looks at me, knowing I am being real and sarcastic at the same time. He inhales a puff from his cigarette then says, "Someday. When I get my life together."

I hope that will be soon, I think to myself, knowing that Mr. Pineapple has been down for 12 years.

There are nearly 4,100 lifers—men, women, and children—as young as 14 who have received sentences of life imprisonment (without the possibility of parole). As years go by, many of them have reformed their lives. They have educated themselves, learned to use rational decision-making, and no longer pose a threat to the safety of society. Many among them are meritorious lifers who have earned a second chance, capable of living outside prison as productive, law-abiding citizens. For them, however, executive clemency has ceased to be a possibility. Society is so hellbent on vengeance that it forgets to be compassionate and forgiving, nurturing the goal of healing.

Although we lifers are a unique group of prisoners, we are nonetheless individuals in our own right. Whatever decisions we make as a collective, organized body, each and every one of us is responsible for the decisions we make in our personal lives. We are not perfect. We make mistakes and, as time goes on, learn from our mistakes. In our attempts to survive the pangs of our incarceration and rediscover our human qualities, we sometimes fall like children learning to walk. Yet lifers, unlike any other group of prisoners I know, always pick themselves up and try again, until they have learned to master their lives.

In my view, the prospect of hope should be a fundamental right protected by our U.S. Constitution. We all need hope in our lives. We lifers have been told for a very long time that someday things will change for us, yet no substantial changes have taken place. Instead, our hopes to earn even a well-deserved second chance have in recent years diminished to nonexistence. We can no longer survive on false promises that yield nothing but false hopes.

To many people, lifers are nothing more than convicted murderers. They fail to realize that although we are being punished for the unlawful taking of another human being's life, we are men, women and children with the inalienable right to redeem ourselves. In many other states, lifers are given that chance and are granted the privilege of consideration for parole. Pennsylvania lifers respectfully ask society to extend that same privilege to those who have earned it by their own merit.

Lifers are like a bowl of fruit. As human beings, we are a product of life and possess the ability to absorb and provide nourishment. When properly nurtured, we can develop into ripe pieces of fruit, each with a different flavor—some delicious, some not. When neglected, we become bruised and spoiled, unfit for human consumption. Pick out the fruits that you do like, and you will find that there are many of us who can refresh the taste of society.

Endnote

1. Eastern State Penitentiary, located in Philadelphia, was the first penitentiary built in the United State in 1829. It was officially closed in 1971 and is now periodically open for tours. ✦

Chapter 29

Joshua

Joshua was a tall, thin boy with short dark hair. He had just arrived at SCI-Huntingdon, where the "hunting is done." He stood with his back against a cement wall, his eyes swollen with the apprehension of lurking dangers, focused on the tiers of cells above him. As I watched him, there was no doubt in my mind that he was scared. All young boys like Joshua are scared, especially those who grew up in the suburbs where their parents shielded them from diversity. I sensed his fear because I too once stood against that cold wall, contemplating the ultimate question of reality: *What have I done to myself?*

I walked up to Joshua, who reminded me of myself, and extended a hand in friendship. We introduced ourselves, and he seemed a bit relieved to find someone "normal" to communicate with. Of course, I understood completely. When I was growing up, I used to hear stories of prisons where some butt-ugly "Bubba" lived to prey on the young boys who entered his lair. Tales of fighting, rape, and even murder instilled in me a deep-rooted fear of such places. I knew that Joshua had heard these stories too, and that we probably shared the same sentiment: Prisons were not meant for people like us.

He lived on C-Block for a few days, and we started going to the dining hall and yard together. Joshua had been privileged to grow up in a wealthy family. His education had far surpassed mine, and I considered him to be a wellspring of knowledge. He was polite and well mannered, a product of his upbringing. When I found out that he was a lifer like myself, I could not help but wonder how such a nice kid could end up like this.

183

Sensing that he could trust me, Joshua admitted that he had murdered two people in his neighborhood while under the influence of drugs. He was now burdened with an unbearable grief and remorse for what he had done. "I know I've got to make up for what I did," he confided. "I've got to make things right again, somehow." I understood how he felt. In time, I shared my story with him as well.

Shortly, Joshua was transferred to another block, but we would see each other from time to time. He seemed to be adjusting to his new lifestyle, at least better than I had done. He soon found an enjoyable job, building and repairing engines in the Automotive Shop. He began to lift weights and told me that he was writing a book. He never revealed what he was writing about, only that he had filled at least seven composition books. He encouraged me to write down my thoughts in a daily journal. The idea appealed to me, and in time I too began writing.

Joshua often spoke about his family, how much he loved them. He was devoted to his engineer father, adored his baby sister, and considered his mother "the greatest mom in the world." He once told me in private, "I let them all down." To me, his voice conjured the image of a beautiful butterfly screaming with pain.

During a Christmas visit when food was allowed from visitors, Joshua's family brought him some shrimp. "I love my family!" he later exclaimed, nearly hugging me. I could see the sadness in his heart, the agony he was trying to hide.

We both passed our GED tests, Joshua scoring very high. At the graduation ceremony, I briefly met the family who seemed so proud of their son and watched how Joshua and his parents tried to make the best of the moment. My own father was unable to attend the ceremony, and I envied Joshua's family support. When it came time to say goodbye, Joshua nearly cried as he hugged his family. His mother looked him straight in the eyes and reassured him that they would always be there for him. "We love you." Joshua and I left together and returned to our housing units, both of us in deep silence.

As time went on, the tall thin boy became more muscular with a weightlifter's build. Our friendship grew more distant, as Joshua befriended a bunch of prisoners whom I did not like nor trusted. He confided to me later that he was back on drugs again, because he had a hard time dealing with prison experiences. "This place is not normal" were his last words to me.

*   *   *

Subsequently transferred to SCI-Frackville, I thought about Joshua from time to time. Years later, I picked up an issue of *Graterfriends*[1] and discovered in an article that Joshua had committed suicide. He was found hanging in his cell. Tears streamed down my face from my grief for Joshua's family, whose lives were no doubt shattered.

The story did not end here, however. The article also revealed that Joshua had expressed his troubles and state of depression to both his girlfriend and other prisoners. Witnesses had seen him collecting pharmaceutical drugs, possibly for a future overdose attempt. His girlfriend had notified the administrative staff of his bouts with depression. His inmate friends had even warned the sergeant and the housing-unit guards that he was a serious candidate for suicide.

Despite all this awareness of his condition, Joshua was neither referred to a staff psychologist nor moved to a cell on the bottom tier where he could be more easily observed. In other words, his suicide might have been prevented had prison officials cared enough to take a few minimal, obvious steps.

Upon his death, no prison administrator contacted Joshua's immediate family to break the news, nor did they offer their condolences. Instead, a prison nurse called Joshua's mother and bluntly informed her: "Your son is dead." No words of sympathy, no apology for their inability to prevent his suicide. While his mother was still in shock, trying to comprehend or deny the truth of these incredibly harsh words, the nurse simply asked: "Where do you want us to send the body?"

*   *   *

Most lifers and other long-term prisoners contemplate suicide from time to time. Whether one is strong or weak, suicide is the ultimate escape from incarceration. The temptation can be as sweet as euphoria, a final release from the demons that make one's existence unbearable.

Joshua was my friend, a brother among lifers, an artesian spring of knowledge for many inmates. He was kind, loyal, honest, intelligent, articulate, and fun to be around. He was also determined to battle the demons that had haunted him for so long. I could never imagine what evil forces had driven this educated, gentle man to take away innocent lives, for Joshua was by no means an evil person. His soul, it seemed to me, had been suffering long before he had committed his crime. Perhaps he had cried out for help in some small way but, like the beautiful butterfly that screamed, he could not be heard. In the end, the lives of two American families would be forever altered, and the Devil would be blamed.

Joshua was my friend. I will miss him.

> Joshua, Joshua
> Why does thou cry?
> Why does thou scream
> O beautiful butterfly?
> Joshua, Joshua
> Spread your wings to the sky
> For now you are free
> Free to fly.

Endnote

1. This newsletter was once published by a nonprofit organization that provides services to prisoners at SCI-Graterford, a maximum security institution outside Philadelphia. It is now published by the Pennsylvania Prison Society. All inmates are permitted to subscribe to it. ✦

Chapter 30

The Old Man and the Mountain

Sitting on an old wooden bench in Rockview's prison yard, my imagination is captured by the majestic mountain across the valley, out of reach beyond the stainless-steel fences and razor wire. I think of Mosheh (Moses), and how Yahweh had once shown him the Promised Land but told him that he would never set his feet on it. I look to the heavens, wondering if a voice will tell me these same words. Of course, I hear no such words. Perhaps a sign of hope?

The mountain beyond, known as Mount Nittany, is so grand that Hispanic prisoners call it "bonita montaña" (beautiful mountain). Mount Nittany is also part of the story of a life-sentenced prisoner who lived and worked on its slopes for over two decades.

"Mr. Dead-Man-Walking," as I will call him, was a freelance photographer who had just turned 26 years old in 1963, when John F. Kennedy was our president. He served four years in the U.S. Navy and earned an associate degree from the University of Miami in Photographic Arts and Sciences.

For unexplained reasons, he shot and killed a 12-year-old neighbor boy with a .30 caliber pistol. He was soon arrested, tried for first-degree murder, found guilty by a jury, and sentenced to death. During the penalty phase of the trial, however, the prosecutor mistakenly told the jury that if he were to receive a life sentence, he would someday be eligible for parole. In Pennsylvania, lifers are not, nor have they ever been, eligible for parole. The defense attorney appealed, arguing that this influenced the jury to sentence the guilty man to death. The Supreme Court agreed and reduced his sentence from death to life imprisonment.

After serving nine and a half years at Western Penitentiary (SCI-Pittsburgh), Mr. Dead-Man-Walking was transferred in 1972 to SCI-Rockview, where he became one of the original founders of the Pennsylvania Lifers' Association at Rockview. A year later, he was assigned to the Forestry Department located on Mount Nittany, a prison job requiring him to work outside the prison and live in an unlocked trailer on the mountainside. He remained there for the next 23 years, earning an apprenticeship in forestry.

In 1997, however, upon the order of the new Secretary of the Pennsylvania Department of Corrections, lifers given outside clearance were to be returned inside the prisons. Mr. Dead-Man-Walking, like so many lifers, had never tried to escape in the belief that his trustworthiness would one day earn him his freedom.

He was well known and deeply respected by surrounding outside communities as well as by the prison staff. During his entire 40 or more years of incarceration, he never once received a misconduct report, a nearly impossible achievement. Everyone regarded him as a man who had regenerated his life to the point where he richly deserved some kind of executive clemency.

In his quest for redemption, Mr. Dead-Man-Walking petitioned the Pennsylvania Board of Pardons on many occasions, asking them to reduce his sentence to make him eligible for parole. He was granted three public hearings. Each time, the victim's family attended the hearing but did not oppose his release. The prosecutor from his trial was now a judge, however, so of course he opposed the commutation.

Despite this hurdle, the Board of Pardons twice approved Mr. Dead-Man-Walking for clemency. On both occasions, two state governors (one a Democrat, the other a Republican) reviewed the petition but refused to sign it. Neither gave any reason for their denial, leaving him in the dark as to what more he had to do to receive a second chance. Recent governors have vowed never to commute the sentence of any lifer, so Mr. Dead-Man-Walking has not bothered to petition the Board of Pardons again. Yet, he still hopes that one day a more understanding governor will save his life while he still has it in him. We all hope so, too.

Mr. Dead-Man-Walking, 65 years old at the time of this writing, has now served 41 years of his life sentence. He works inside the prison Cannery as a clerk.

*   *   *

A young lifer, only 21 years old, comes to me for advice on a legal matter. He is one of those rebel youths whose inappropriate behavior frequently earns him misconduct reports, so he spends a lot of time on cell restriction or in the RHU. I have encouraged him to stay out of trouble and focus his energies on more positive activities, such as supporting the PLAR.

In the midst of our conversation, the young lifer brings up the subject of Mr. Dead-Man-Walking. "Look at him," he tells me, "that old man spent over 40 years of his life in here. He's a model inmate who causes no problems—and where did all his good behavior get him? Nowhere!" I must admit, he poses a challenging question. What can I possibly say to convince him that there is hope for him, that he must be willing to change his own life?

"You must never give up on hope," I insist. "If we lifers ever wanna have an opportunity for freedom, we must do those things that will help us earn that chance. Sure, it's true, hope seems nonexistent right now, but if we want to change that, we must be willing to fight for it. We can't afford to feel defeated and give up our lives. That means doing your best to stay misconduct-free, get your GED, and take advantage of every opportunity that will help improve your life skills. That's what you need to do. Build up your life, because nobody else is gonna do it for you. Arguing and cussing at the guards like you do won't help you rebuild your life—it only helps to destroy it!"

"You may be right, but until I see things change, I'm gonna do what I think is best for me."

"What's that?"

"Hustlin'. Makin' money. Doin' what I gotta do to survive. I'm a soldier."

As he turns to leave, I explain that prisoners only become real soldiers when they are able to build up their lives with as much education as possible, then use that knowledge to change themselves and their circumstances. But he just walks away from me, flinging his arms dismissively over his head.

No matter what I tell this young man, he stubbornly refuses to adhere to my counsel. I figure to myself, in time he will probably learn through experience as I did. I only hope it will not be too late for him.

From time to time, I still see that young lifer, rowdy and careless as ever. I compare him to Mr. Dead-Man-Walking—who is still actively involved in the PLAR, presently serving as treasurer on the Executive Board.

Each and every day, I notice that beautiful mountain, today covered with a lush carpet of verdant green. In the fall, its trees will turn a picturesque yellow, orange, red, and brown. In the winter, the mountain will be bare, sometimes blanketed with snow. I watch the mountain change with the seasons, and I think about all the lifers who too have to change year after year.

What Is Life?

Life is being alive
Life is being able to live
Life is growing
Life is learning
Life is being able to make mistakes
Life is both perfect and imperfect
Life is being able to be happy
Life is being able to build
Life is realizing our own personal potentials
Life is being able to transform time into
    achievements and blessings.
Life is love
Life is being able to love
Life is forgiving
Life is being able to forgive
Life is being able to raise a family
Life is being able to produce more life
Life is spiritual
Life is precious
Life is not confined, but lived
Life is being able to do all those things that make life
    worth living
And if one cannot live life
What then is the purpose of living? ✦

Part X
Family

Chapter 31

Thinking of You

In times that pass me by,
Often I think of you,
Memories,
The only possessions that I truly own.
As time goes by so slowly,
Often I think of you,
Emotions,
Caressing the loneliness that I truly feel.
When time is all I have,
Often I think of you,
Wondering,
If I will ever be the same.
The memories are possessions I cannot sell,
The emotions that loneliness cannot buy,
The wondering will always be the same,
Often I think of you.

One summer day, I lie on my bed thinking about my family. My father, a former U.S. Marine, just lost his job working at a textile factory that recently closed its doors. He was *semper fidelis*, "always faithful" like a true Marine, working for the same company for 28 years. Though too proud to collect unemployment benefits, he had no choice in the matter. I decide to give him a phone call this afternoon.

Under normal circumstances, I usually only call home in an emergency, because the state prisons operate on a collect-call system that burdens my family and friends with paying for the costs. Not only has the phone company tripled its collect-call rate[1] for phone calls from state prisons, but outgoing calls are now monitored and electronically recorded. Communication by mail is more economical. This time, however, I want to call my father for three reasons: to console him over the loss of his job, to let him know that I love him, and just to hear his voice.

Prisoners are required to sign up to use the telephone. This helps the guards keep track of phone time, so that each prisoner is allowed an equal opportunity to call out. Scheduling varies at each SCI. Even though I am not signed up this afternoon, I plan to ask permission for access to a phone.

Two phones are available on the housing unit. Neither one is occupied, so I ask the guard politely for phone privilege. "Ask the sarge," he replies. I try again at the sergeant's desk. "Is anyone else scheduled?" the sergeant asks the guard. The guard looks at the sign-up sheet. "Yeah, but I saw him go to the yard." The sergeant turns to me with a shrug. "I don't care. Ten minutes."

Ten minutes is good enough for me. I go to the telephone, pick up the receiver, wipe it with my brown shirt, and dial my father collect. "Hello?" I say right away.

"Yeah, Jim," comes my father's welcome voice.

"I just called to see how you were doing. I received your letter a week ago."

"Yeah, the company closed down. I'm collecting unemployment, but it doesn't pay much."

"Gonna find another job?"

"One of the guys I know has a private business. He offered me a job. I thought about it, but I don't want to work no more. I want to retire."

"Yeah, but you can't collect Social Security until you're at least 62 years old."

"I know. The company offered to send me to a cooking school, but I'm not interested. Betty has a job. She'll take care of me."

"So what are you doing?"

"I did some touch-up painting. Relaxing. Your sister called, and she wants me to tell you that she loves you. She's having another baby."

"Another baby? Dad, why is she doing this?"

"I know, I know. I told her. She's like you, thick-headed and never listens. It's her life, Jim."

"I'll write to her. Anything else going on?"

"Well, I need a new roof. I told you about calling. The phone company's ripping us off. I can't afford to waste any money. Things are tight."

"I understand. I just wanted to make sure you were all right."

The guard motions that I have one minute remaining.

"I'm alright. How about you?"

"Keeping strong. You just keep praying."

"I pray for you every night."

"I gotta go, Dad. I love you always."

"Love you, too, Jim."

We never say goodbye, a part of me always desperate to talk with my father forever. There was a time in our lives when we hardly ever talked or expressed our love for one another, even though as a child it was the one thing that I craved the most. My father was a great family provider, making sure we had a roof over our heads, good food on the table, and nice clothes to wear. In that respect, I can honestly say that my sister and I had it better than most kids I grew up with. Now for the first time in our lives, we finally talk to each other and express our true feelings like father and son.

I hang up and thank the sergeant, who waves me away dismissively. My brief moment of happiness may have registered on him, but he has seven more hours of duty time to put up with and probably couldn't care less.

No phone call, letter, or visit can ever substitute for the years that my father and I took for granted. This is the last phone call we will have, given the high cost of collect calling and the institutional invasion of our privacy by the prison's newly installed monitoring and recording system. Today, at least, I feel grateful just to hear my father's real voice, rather than some distant memory in my head.

* * *

Today is visiting day, a very special day for me. After breakfast, I shower and spend half an hour grooming myself in preparation. I check my new haircut in the mirror and tell myself, what a handsome guy. I only hope my visitors will be as impressed. Okay. I am ready. So, where are they? Not even five minutes go by, and already I feel the anxiety of waiting. Ten minutes. I hope nothing has happened to them. I convince myself to remain calm. After all, I have been down this road too many times before—no use getting stressed out over a visit. They will be here. I hope.

I have waited a whole year for this moment. The loudspeaker message finally comes: "BQ-3769 . . . Paluch . . . you have a visit." My anxiety dissolves instantly away, replaced by happy excitement. I quickly lock up my cell and run down to the bubble to retrieve my visiting pass.

In a changing room, I take off my clothes and put on a brown jumpsuit that I must zipper up from my belly to my neck, a necessary security precaution. I replace my boots with a pair of leisure sneakers also provided by the staff. I place my personal belongings into a locker, then hurry out into the visiting room.

My visitors are just coming through the civilian entrance. My sister takes one look at me and turns away to cry. As I hug her, she hands me the most beautiful gift of human life I have ever seen: my 1-year-old nephew, Alex. I hold him up over my head, and he smiles down at me. I know right then and there that we have become the best of friends.

As I cradle Baby Alex in my arms, my father and my uncle arrive. I greet my father with a kiss and my uncle with a handshake. This is the last time I ever see my uncle, who will pass away shortly after this visit.

We find a place to sit down. Whatever I wanted to discuss with my family has now escaped me. Little is said during the four-hour visit, as my mind and my heart are totally focused on Baby Alex. His beautiful, cream-colored skin is as soft as his sky-blue eyes. He grabs the glasses on my face, but when I gently say, "Alex . . . no," he listens. The sign of an intelligent child.

Later, as I talk to my father Alex sticks his fingers inside my mouth. I manage to dissuade him, sharing his merry laughter. Like any baby, he sometimes sits still but mostly squirms and squiggles. Never in my entire life have I ever held a baby in my arms, let alone one that I was so completely unwilling to give up.

The PLAR has purchased children's books for the visiting room, so that inmates can read a book to a child in an effort to promote good reading and family values. These books are allowed to be taken home for the child's benefit. I show Alex six different books to choose from. He selects *The Lion King* and carries it in his tiny hands with remarkable dexterity. Everything about Alex makes me realize how amazing he really is. I am proud to be his uncle.

When it is time for my family to leave, Alex has fallen asleep in my arms. I surrender him to his mother and kiss him goodbye. I yearn so much to take him back to my cell, but of course that is impossible. There will be other visits, I assure myself, perhaps even a time when Alex and I will be together in the free world. I kiss my sister and father farewell, then embrace my uncle.

During the past 11 years of my incarceration, never was I more happy than the day I met "Alex the Great."

*   *   *

Today, my work supervisor allows his slaves to leave their work detail a little earlier than usual. I grab my belongings and wait for a brief pat-down search by my supervisor, then I am electronically scanned by a guard before I head back to the housing unit. Only one thing occupies my mind at the moment, as it has for the past two weeks: a letter from my father.

For the large majority of prisoners, receiving mail is the next best thing to a visit. A handwritten letter from a family member, pen pal, or girlfriend is a blessing—to me an act of love. It makes me feel good to know someone cares enough to take a few minutes of their time to let me know their thoughts. When I get no mail, especially for days at a time, my anxiety reaches frustrating proportions.

Back at the housing unit, I immediately go to the block bulletin board where the mail list is posted. A crowd of inmates usually waits in line to view the list, but not today—not one prisoner at the bulletin board. I look for my number, listed in alphanumerical order. "BQ-3769." Yes! I got mail!

I rush to the bubble and politely ask the guard for my mail. "Paluch. BQ-3769," I announce with anticipation. As he fingers through the mail, I notice that most prisoners' mail has already been distributed and there is little left. The guard finds a letter and hands it to me through a window opening. It is indeed from my father. I beeline excitedly to my cell, kick off my boots, close my door, and feverishly open my letter.

My father writes to me at least once a month, knowing how I look forward to the letters as a source of comfort and support. Although we have been separated by terrible circumstances, we both know that we love each other unconditionally. Ironically, it took my imprisonment for both of us to realize this important truth.

This particular letter has been anticipated even more so, because it contains a money order. Three weeks ago, I wrote to my father and asked for some financial assistance. I just started a new prison job, so I have been without any idle pay. I needed to purchase such cosmetics as shampoo, soap, deodorant, toothpaste, etc., as well as stationery supplies.

It truly grieves me to ask my father for this kind of help, and I know it is not his obligation to relieve my financial burdens. When I ask for money, it is only in an emergency where I cannot obtain it from my own efforts. Of all my friends and family members, none have ever asked me if I needed financial assistance, even though they know that I always need help. I am at a point in my incarceration, however, where I realize that I will not refuse any help that is offered.

My father writes the following [bracketed words are mine]:

> James,
>
> Hope to find you in good health and spirits. Good visit for everyone. Alex is a beautiful boy in every way. Very healthy and getting big. Good-looking devil. Your glasses look good on you. Send me your old ones [they are broken]. See if we can find frames for them. Do they have to be sent from where you get them from or what? My Eagles [his favorite NFL team] did good this year, maybe better next year. Let George and I know when the [PLAR] banquet is in May or June? Give me the date and price. The Brass Rail [a hometown restaurant] has closed. The one on Lehigh Street is still open. If George don't have anything planned that date, March 21st, 10:00–12:00 [a reference to my father and uncle attending the annual PA CURE[2]]? Sending you a money order. Spend it wisely. See you soon.
>
> Love,
>
> Your Father

His letters are usually as short as the lives we live. But in my heart, they are as long as my memory, and my life, remains.

* * *

Christmas morning, 4:30 A.M. Everyone else is sleeping as I write these words. For some, it is Christmas; for many others, just another routine day. Today for a change, the heating on the five tiers of the East and West wings is relatively comfortable, so we do not have to endure freezing temperatures.

5:00 A.M. I am still the only creature stirring. Even the mice are sleeping. Growing up as a Catholic, I was blessed to live in a home where Christmas was celebrated in style. The entire house was decorated, colored lights blinking from windows. A six-foot artificial Christmas tree towered in the living room, adorned with Mom's special "Campbell's Kids" glass ball ornaments. A silver bell hanging from the chandelier played Christmas songs. Bayberry candles burned their seasonal aroma. Cookies, cakes, and all manner of delicious candies abounded. All day long, my parents played their Christmas records. Nobody could sing them better than Burl Ives; one of my favorites is *Silver and Gold*.

Santa Claus, snowmen, garlands, and gift wrap. But here in present-day reality, it is guards, bars, fences, and concrete.

6 A.M. Standing count. As I wait for the guards to pass me by, I recall the plastic bag of holiday treats they issued last night. Each year, inmates are given the opportunity to use Inmate General Welfare Fund (IGWF) money to purchase holiday-treat packages. This year, the IGWF Committee purchased and distributed sample-sized packets of meat, cheese, potato chips, Crunch and Munch, cookies, crackers, and a candy cane for every prisoner. The institution contributed holiday cookies made in the Culinary Department and homemade chocolate fudge. The Pennsylvania Lifers' Association at Rockview chipped in with a pair of white tube socks for each inmate.

The gesture is greatly appreciated, more so here than at SCI-Frackville. At that prison, the inmates' holiday-treat package consists of a sample-sized portion of shampoo, a hotel-sized bar of soap, a cheap washcloth, a small tube of Japanese-made toothpaste, a small packet of Fig Newtons, and a tiny box of raisins that you can swallow in one bite.

Passing by, one of the guards pauses to say "Merry Christmas." As a Yahwist, I no longer celebrate Christmas, but this guard is a decent type whose tone is genuine. "Thank you," I reply respectfully.

In another hour, our housing unit will be called for the morning breakfast line. I am a bit tired, so I go back to bed. I pray that when I wake up, I will smell my father's breakfast cooking and hurry downstairs for the traditional opening of gifts.

7:15 A.M. The blaring breakfast bell awakens me to the stark reality of my cell. As usual, I go through the same motions of every day of every year—clothes, boots, cell lockup, then downstairs to the dining hall. Instead of that gift-wrapped Remington electric razor I imagined opening, the only things I unwrap this Christmas are two hard-boiled eggs. I sneak two pieces of stale toast into my pocket for the sparrows outside. Normally, they just swipe up the bread and fly away, but today they stay on the ground and look up at me as if to say "Thanks."

As I enter the block, the silence I heard early this morning has succumbed to the usual cacophony of madness. Inmates seem cheerful this morning, and no fights arise. Someone rips up a book and drops the pieces from an upper tier like holiday confetti. The sergeant's loudspeaker bellows "Thank you," and I hear a few chuckles. Nevertheless, the guards look depressed, a few complaining about having to work today. Holidays take a toll on everyone, especially Christmas.

Because of the holiday-treat packages, there is more trash around the housing unit than usual. Some men have no respect for others, nor for themselves. Despite the holiday spirit, these malcontents have neither "peace on earth" nor good will. They are miserable and want everyone else to know it. Like the surrounding noise, we lifers have learned to drown out their wretched displays of sorrow. After all, this is a special day . . . or is it?

A feeble Christmas tree stands on the block, decorated only with silver garland. Some of the men, mainly Christians, have homemade Christmas trees in their cells, usually constructed from cardboard or paper. A few even have small gifts under their trees and exchange them with their spiritual brothers. Regardless of the most dehumanizing conditions, some prisoners manage to overcome their burden and stay in touch with their humanity.

At an institution like SCI-Frackville, the guards would most likely destroy any cell Christmas trees and issue misconduct reports for possession of contraband. At SCI-Rockview, however, prison officials respect an inmate's right to be human; a right that most prisoners appreciate and try not to abuse.

Holidays are also a time for bouts of sadness and depression. Inmates can become more irritable around the winter holidays, evidenced by frequent mood swings. Recently, a friend and I were playing a game of acey-ducey after a visit with his parents and sister that seemed to lift his spirits. The next day, however, he refused to play another game and appeared withdrawn. He just did not want to be bothered. This type of behavior happens often during the holidays.

Commissary sales seem to boom this time of year, inmates buying more food than they normally need, probably as a panacea for depression and coping with circumstances beyond their control. A prison's tradition of distributing holiday-treat packages helps to counter the low morale among its inmates.

Like everything else in prison, inmates adjust and adapt to their hardships during holidays as best as they can. The stronger one's constitution, the better one is equipped to deal with negative emotions. The biggest factors that contribute to sadness, depression, and withdrawal are thoughts of preincarceration. Society can deprive us of our freedom, but it cannot take away our lasting memories.

My deepest sadness arises whenever I remember Christmas with my family and friends: building a snowman, riding a sled, or kissing a girlfriend under the mistletoe, which makes my prison reality all the more difficult to endure. For many inmates, such treasured moments from the past are suspended. For us lifers, on the other hand, old memories remain as strong as our undying hopes.

Endnotes

1. In 2002, the Lobbyist Coalition was able to get legislature introduced and passed that has significantly lowered the costs of making collect calls from Pennsylvania state prisons.
2. "Pennsylvania Citizens United for Rehabilitation of Errants" is a nonprofit organization that provides support and advocacy for prisoners and their families in Pennsylvania. The above-mentioned rally takes place each year at the Capitol rotunda in Harrisburg, PA;

its purpose is to bring legislative attention to criminal justice reforms. ✦

Chapter 32

A Sad Day for
Mr. Strawberry

On a typically cold winter evening, block activities have commenced. I previously made a promise to my inmate friend Mr. Strawberry that I would help him review his math for the GED test he is scheduled to take next week. When the block-out bell rings, I hurry downstairs to find a warm, well-lighted study table before they are all occupied.

As I approach the front of the block, the outside door is open and a sudden burst of winter chill hits me in the face. The weather is freezing outside, the sky dark.

I am able to reserve a table seat, and soon Mr. Strawberry arrives. He asks me how my day has gone. "The usual," I reply. He shares a joke with me, and I get a good laugh. "Okay," I say, interrupting our fun, "time to work on these fractions you're having problems with."

Mr. Strawberry is in his early 40s, a lifer from Philadelphia. A fairly big man, he is quite the gentleman despite his burly frame. When he first came here, he could not read or write. After six years of prison, he has learned the basics of reading, writing, spelling, and math, attaining the fifth-grade reading level required by the Pennsylvania Department of Corrections. But he wants to earn his GED so he can learn to decipher law books in the prison library, which require a 12th-grade reading level or higher.

Mr. Strawberry recently had his final direct appeal denied by the Pennsylvania Superior Court, and his court-appointed lawyer failed to file allocatur with the Pennsylvania Supreme Court. The direct-appeal brief that his lawyer did file for him, like the majority of legal briefs prepared on behalf of indigent prisoners, raised frivolous legal issues. Mr. Strawberry is now trying to learn as much as he can to save his own life. Sadly, by the time he masters the language of Commonwealth law, which can take years, it may be too late for him. By then, his legal remedies may have already expired. This common dilemma often applies to most of Pennsylvania's state prisoners.

Mr. Strawberry, however, has the potential to gain a wealth of knowledge beyond legal expertise to fortify himself with valuable personal and professional life skills. Without the will to better himself, the realities of his incarceration will desensitize his mind and lead to all-consuming delusions. Mr. Strawberry understands this inherent truth when he tells me:

"I don't want to become like those other guys in here. They are *totally unaware*."

We have been working on the division of fractions for at least half an hour, when the bubble loudspeaker announces, "XA-8953, Strawberry, come to the desk."

"That's me," he says as he rises. "I'll be right back."

Mr. Strawberry leaves his materials on the table and heads to the bubble. I watch him, as the guard speaks with him through the window. Instead of rejoining me, he hastens away to a phone to make a collect call. Something is amiss, I suspect, given that unscheduled calls are only authorized in an emergency. Mr. Strawberry is on the phone for at least 15 minutes before he hangs up. He hurries back to our table to retrieve his paperwork.

"What's up?" I ask.

"Bof, I gotta go back to my cell. We'll do this another time."

*   *   *

Shortly, I learn the sad news: Mr. Strawberry's mother has died suddenly. She lived too far away to visit, though his sister had recently promised to bring her to the prison. I remember Mr. Strawberry telling me that his mom baked the best homemade bread in the world, and that Grandpa Stroehman would have gone bankrupt had his mother gone into business. I do not have to see Mr. Strawberry in his cell to know that he is probably crying right now, hurting badly.

In 1991, I too lost my mother while incarcerated in the Philadelphia Detention Center awaiting trial. I know what Mr. Strawberry is going through. It may take a very long time before his pain subsides, but I know that he must somehow find the strength to carry on.

I still see Mr. Strawberry from time to time, though not as often as before. He has become somewhat withdrawn and less sociable. The last time I spoke with him, I learned that he passed his GED and still has plans to continue his education. I never ask about his mother or how he is dealing with his loss. However, I always pray for him.

Lifers feel helpless when they lose a loved one, especially a close family member. At present, we are not permitted to attend the funeral or wake of an immediate family member, given that we are considered too much of a security risk. A perpetual heartache exists inside us with the knowledge that, as time goes on, we will lose more and more loved ones, until our outside support system dwindles away and ceases to exist.

Throughout the years, many lifers lose their entire families. Without that blood connection, it becomes harder to survive and even more difficult to believe in hope.

Totally Unaware

At the time of my arrest I was totally unaware
Reality did not exist nor did I care
My heart being numb yet deceitfully lacerated
A mind untamed and previously incarcerated
I fell a victim to an indescribable sin
And hated myself because of the feelings within
Nobody knew that I suffered inside
From all the grief that I tried to hide
The meaning of life I placed on a shelf
And I lost all the respect that I had for myself
Although I knew the values of both right and wrong
I never realized what I had until it was gone
"Hey there boy, what did you do?"
A piece of life's puzzle I wish I knew
What can a prison do to me

If a man is aware that he is totally free?
Yet not for me, but for my indecision
Being unaware had sent me to prison
A sentence of death in this case no lesser
Under a restraint of a system I call my Oppressor
Living amongst those labeled demented and insane
I now realize I was the only one to blame
If only I had been aware from the start
And disciplined myself with a pure heart
All this pain would have been a void
Two more lives therefore enjoyed
No more denial or hating myself still
Nothing in my heart would cause me to kill
I was once confused and made a bad mistake
In revenge it's my life they now forsake
My only hope comes from the faith I believe
In awareness the key I need to relieve
Please forgive me and redeem the soul I mend
Restore my life and cause this pain to end
I was a guilty child, lonely, and in despair
I was just 18 years old and *totally unaware.* ✦

Chapter 33

A Lifer's Dad

James A. Paluch, Sr.

Never in a million years would I have ever thought that my own son would one day go to prison, nor in my worst nightmares ever believe that he would be charged with the crime of murder. So when my wife had told me that our son was in a Philadelphia County prison because he was arrested for murder, I did not believe it. When I saw it on a television news station, I was devastated.

At the time my son was arrested, I was not financially capable of securing him a paid attorney. My wife at the time was diagnosed with ovarian cancer, and our insurance was barely paying for all the medical expenses. However, I supported my son the best that I could and made certain that my wife and I made trips to visit with him to let him know that we were there for him. During visits, my son appeared to be medicated and was not his normal self. His eyes that were once filled with love, humor, and the focus to achieve were replaced with the glassy, dejected look of depression and confusion. As we drove back home after our visit, his mother cried during the entire trip. All we could do was pray for our son.

As if there was not enough grief in my life over the possibility of losing my wife and over my son's arrest, my heart suffered its worst attack when I learned from my son's court-appointed lawyer that the district attorney was seeking the death penalty against him. I never shared this information with my wife, who would pass away in the next few months. Not only had I lost my beloved wife of 19 years, but I was also facing the reality of losing my son. I wanted to do everything within my power to help save my son's life, but I did not know what else I could do but pray. I felt helpless.

At trial, I testified that my son's character was loving, peaceful, and good-natured. He was very educated, and had aspirations of becoming a landscaper, for which he went to school. My son always had a decent job, even when he was in school. Always a lady's man, he was involved in a long-term relationship with a girlfriend. He was an excellent kicker and punter for his high school varsity football team. And yes, like any All-American kid growing up, he had his problems and difficulties with life. But he was both a friend and inspiration to all those who knew him.

When the jury sentenced my son to life imprisonment, I was somewhat relieved that at least he was not sentenced to death. Yet after I found out that my son is not eligible for parole, I came to the realization that a life sentence is no better than a death sentence, if not worse. I had read in a few newspapers that the Governor had signed death warrants for death-row prisoners, but I had never before heard of those prisoners, sentenced to life imprisonment, dying in prison from either suicide or an old-age sickness. When my son showed me the statistics of life-sentenced prisoners who died in prison compared to those who were executed on death row, I became convinced that a life sentence was nothing more than a silent sentence of death.

My son had no right to take away another human being's life. And even though the Commonwealth of Pennsylvania believes that this crime was a first-degree homicide, nobody, not even the state, should have the right to take away his life. I feel deep sympathy for the family of the person whose life was tragically ended by my son, and I hope and pray that instead of hating my son they will hate what he did and forgive him. He is not a monster, and although his crime should never be condoned, he is a human being with redemptive values. Taking away his life is not going to bring back the life he took away, nor it is it going to make our society a better or safer place to live. My son may deserve to be punished for his crime, but "Vengeance is Mine," sayeth Yahweh.

Over the years, I have seen my son grow and mature. I still visit with him, although it may only be once or twice a year because he is so far away from home. We write to each other at least once a month, and when I do not receive a letter by a certain time, I wonder if he is okay. Being that he is in a state prison, I often worry about his personal safety. I pray not only for him, but that I will never receive a phone call from prison officials that something terrible has happened to him. I want to be able to live to someday see my son come home where he belongs. Until then, I will always be there for him. ✦

Chapter 34

A Lifer's Mom

Joyce Upchurch

I am the mother of two lifers and have been for the past 20 years. Those 20 years have had many different feelings for me.

It all began on a cold January day. I came home from work like any other ordinary day, not knowing what was lying ahead for me and my family. Around 9 P.M., I heard a knock at my front door. Dressed in my nightclothes, I answered the door only to find the police. In a matter of moments, the entire house was full of police before I even knew what was happening. I had always believed that these things happen to other people, but not to me. The many times I have watched television or read the newspapers and heard about these things, my heart had always gone out to the mothers and families who went through these experiences.

For days, I believed that I would wake up at any time, hoping that this was just a dream. I wanted so desperately to speak to anyone who was willing to listen, just to be reassured that there existed a little hope. In time, there would be periods when I just wanted to be alone. When my sons were found guilty of murder in a court of law, they received the penalty of life imprisonment, a sentence that is not parolable in Pennsylvania. The thought of having both my sons condemned to die in prison made me seriously depressed for some time. Somewhere out there was a family grieving the loss of their loved one, while I too was grieving the loss of my sons. It was as though my life unexpectedly shattered—altered through no fault of my own. I worked in a coffee shop where lots of people came in.

They too saw that I was not the same person they knew before this tragedy happened. It was only through my spiritual strength that I was able to overcome the depression. Despite the sadness and loneliness that I felt inside, I still had a husband, four other children, and grandchildren who needed me to be there for them. It was not easy, but I just could not give up.

The eldest of my two sons had a wife and three children, one of whom was just six months old at the time, and two other boys aged 3 and 4. For a while, his wife and I would visit him at the prison. When he was transferred to another prison far away from home, I felt responsible for his family, making sure that they were receiving food and clothing to make it by. However, my daughter-in-law soon gave up on him and filed for divorce. When my husband retired, we moved away to the mountains. Within time, my son's children lost touch with their father. Today, my oldest grandchild has a son of his own who none of us have ever seen.

The youngest of my two sons was never married. It pains him and his entire family that he will never be given the chance to have a family of his own. While in prison, he was diagnosed with multiple sclerosis and has had some bad days dealing with this debilitating disease. For a long time the prison did not give him the medications that he needed, but now he is receiving them. He educates himself about the disease by reading books and other materials related to multiple sclerosis. My heart aches for him.

At one time, both my sons were in two different prisons. When it came time to visit them, I felt like I was being torn in two different directions. I felt so frustrated. These were the times when I could be hurt so deep. I consider myself to be just like any other mother who has unconditional love for her children.

For the past five years, the boys have been at the same prison, for which I am truly grateful. My daughter and I can now visit them together at the same time. There are also two ladies from my church who go with us when they can. I am also proud of what nice men the boys have become. Both are active members of their lifers' organization, and one is working very hard at producing a newsletter. The other is busy tracing our family genealogy back to the 1400s.

I have always been a person who enjoys life and making other people laugh. There is never a day that goes by without my doing what I can to save the lives of my two sons. I often think of and pray for those family members who lost their loved ones to violence. I understand the pain they feel, and I wonder if they can feel mine. There are times when I ask myself if there was something that I could have done to prevent these circumstances from happening. What could I have done differently? Time cannot be changed, so for me life goes on as I continue to live with the pain, and the hope of one day being reunited with my sons. One day at a time. ✦

Chapter 35

A Wife Doing Life

Dianna L. Hollis

In 1982, little did I know that when I fell in love with my husband Mr. Peach, a lifer, I would face so many ups and downs because of his sentence. Our relationship grew from mutual respect and friendship to love, as we worked together in the Dispensary at SCI-Camp Hill.

Being married to a prisoner, especially a lifer, is a very difficult situation. It is a very lonely life that causes a feeling of emptiness deep within. He is not there when I return home from a hard day's work to discuss how my day went or to have someone to vent my feelings to. There is no one to wait for, no one to greet at the door after his day's end.

When a crisis arises, he is not there to comfort me, to hold me, to offer his knowledge and wisdom, or to provide the emotional and spiritual support I need. When I call the institution to ask staff to have him call me, I am oftentimes told I have to go through his counselor, who is gone for the day. If he is given the message, or when he calls home, our phone calls are monitored with no privacy. He is not there to help me with household problems and chores too physically taxing for a woman to complete. He is not there to nurse me when I am sick.

At times, a sense of anger and frustration comes over me, but I have no helpmate to deal with the daily responsibilities that I alone face. Certain times of the year are more difficult than others. I see couples walking in the spring when the trees and grass become green with new life, new beginnings—wishing we could share just the simple things in life that other couples take for granted, feeling envy of others who have the opportunities that we sorely lack.

Christmas is a time to share with your loved ones, but my husband is clearly absent. On New Year's Eve, he is only in my thoughts as a new year begins. I wish he were here to kiss the New Year in, wondering if this year will bring him home.

Being married to an incarcerated man often forces me into secrecy because of people's insensitivity to prisoners in general. It is as though I lead two lives—one that people see and one that is hidden, making up white lies about what I do on my day off when I go to see my husband in a prison visiting room.

My loneliness is enhanced because there are few nonjudgmental people, even family members, with whom I can discuss my relationship. There is always the chance that I will be perceived as "crazy." People are easy to criticize but unwilling to learn about Mr. Peach and the reasons why I am committed to him. At work, it is difficult to hear women talk about plans for their vacations and holidays, the things they have bought their husbands for their birthdays, or vice versa, while having to deal with the reality of my own life. I feel myself being excluded from conversations with people who know my situation, or I probably feel that it is useless to engage in such conversations because of their insensitivity to me.

The financial responsibilities fall completely on my shoulders. From 1983 to the present, I have held two jobs. When Mr. Peach needs anything, it is up to me to supply his needs. I pay the overexcessive telephone rates that I am charged when he makes a collect call from a state prison. Because of the increased costs, we have to talk less often—increasing once again my feeling of loneliness and separation. The costs of weekly visits take a financial toll on me as well. Gas, car maintenance, the high cost of food from the visiting-room vending machines, and photographs are all personal expenses.

It is easy to say, do not visit and do not accept his calls, but those two very things, including Mr. Peach's letters, keep me going from day to day. When I leave him at the end of the visit, I immediately start counting the days until I can see him again. When I have a hectic week, I find comfort in knowing that I will see him soon. It is those visits that restore me, and quite honestly, they are some of the few times when I truly laugh and enjoy myself. I do things and go places, but I constantly feel the sadness and emptiness, that hollow feeling, all because he is not there with me. I picture in my mind how we could be doing things together. I find that even though I am in the free world, I am merely "existing," going through the motions but not living. For me, it is not what you do but who you do it with that matters.

Dealing with the incarceration itself is very stressful, causing physical problems like hypertension for both of us. The threats of bogus misconducts that could separate us permanently, retaliation, racism, and harassment in the visiting room over petty things are constant.

I worry about Mr. Peach's health, because the medical care and treatment he receives is below the standard for those of us out here in society. Medical policies in prison constitute pure negligence. I worry that, should he ever injure himself or have a life-threatening condition, will he get the proper care? I seriously doubt that he will.

I worry about Mr. Peach's safety, should there ever be a riot or a disturbance inside the prison. Will he become an innocent victim? He was supposed to call, I think, and he did not. Is he okay? The anxiety I feel disturbs me, until I am able to hear his voice. Oftentimes, we lose the means to communicate. When I call the prison, the staff is sometimes unwilling or too incompetent to give me the information that I need. There is also the anxiety of a prison lockdown, which happens from time to time. I am never sure when the lockdown will end or when I will be able to visit again. Will it resume on my day off, or must I wait until I have another day off?

As happened four years ago, I worry that he will suddenly be transferred, perhaps farther away from me, because I have spoken out against injustices and wrongs perpetrated within the system. Unfortunately, retaliation and racism are often difficult to prove.

I remember reading about one lifer, Reginald McFadden, who was given the rare gift of freedom via executive clemency, and how he failed. McFadden, who was not a meritorious lifer, was only granted a commutation of his life sentence because he provided testimony against some alleged participants in the 1989 Camp Hill riots. McFadden's undeserved release, then his later crime of rape and murder in New York, has caused deserving Pennsylvania lifers to pay dearly because of the government's irresponsibility.

I think of Mr. Peach's commutation papers sitting on the Governor's desk for a year and a half, waiting for a decision, only to be denied, no reasons given. Yet, someone like McFadden was granted commutation. So now my husband is being held accountable for not only McFadden's criminal actions but for some politicians' and bureaucrats' irresponsible deeds. It haunts me to think that Mr. Peach was just a signature away from freedom. I ask myself, will it ever happen again? I long just to share some of the best years left of our own lives together.

Despite the negatives surrounding my husband's incarceration, our relationship has indeed grown stronger over the years. We have experienced many trials and tribulations, but our love for each other has sustained our marriage. Mr. Peach has great faith, and it is because of our faith in the Creator that we have survived. I have often told him that if he were not the man he is, I would not have stayed in the relationship, because it is too difficult. Consequently, I believe that we know each other better than most married couples do in the free world.

We use most of the time we share together to learn about each other, discussing issues and reading the Holy Scriptures without the distraction of outside influences like television. We have grown in mental love, and each of us usually knows the other's thoughts and feelings—often writing about the same things in our letters. He treats me with respect, and I feel like a special, loved woman. I feel warmth, and I am aglow in his presence. He is my emotional and spiritual support, as well as my advisor in the many hardships that I face, offering his unique wisdom. He has a good sense of humor and he lightens the heaviness I so often feel.

I could never walk away from our love, despite all the negatives. I have devoted myself to him and to our 20 years of marriage. To let another woman reap the rewards of my hardships would be wrong. Perhaps that is selfish on my part, but that is how I feel.

Mr. Peach and I have great faith in the Creator. We believe that if He says, "it shall be," it will be. We pray that He will fulfill our prayers, and that Mr. Peach will come home.

Until then, I too am "doing life." ✦

Part XI

Conclusion

Chapter 36

Forgive Them, Father . . .

Author's Note

At SCI-Huntingdon in 1994, I was asked by an inmate library worker to deliver some legal materials to the B-Block sergeant who supervised Death Row. Inside B-Block, I presented the materials to the sergeant. He was busy, however, and directed me to deliver them directly to the inmate who had requested them: Timothy Ryan.

When I came to Timothy's cell, he thanked me for the legal papers then asked, "Do you accept Jesus Christ as your Lord and Savior?"

I did not want to discuss my personal faith and beliefs, so I replied, "If you're asking me if I am saved . . . yes."

He then asked me what it was like to be in the general population, and if the inmate organization that sells ice cream could ask the administration for permission to sell ice cream to Death Row prisoners. I assured him that I would pass his message on to the organization, which I later did.

Some time later, I was extremely saddened to learn that Timothy Ryan had been executed. Executions in Pennsylvania take place at SCI-Rockview.

The following is a fictionalized account of Timothy Ryan's last day on earth. It is based on interviews I conducted with people at SCI-Rockview who were knowledgeable about executions in general and about this execution in particular. Those people read this account and assured me that it is accurate.

I wrote the account as if it were being told by a correctional officer who had participated in the execution. While some parts of the conversations between Timothy Ryan and the guards are fictionalized, the details of the execution are accurately described as they happen. It is intended to accurately

221

portray what prisoners sentenced to death experience in the last few hours of their lives.

*   *   *

I first met Timothy Ryan at the death house when I was assigned duty to this particular post. Within a few hours, we were able to have a normal conversation, but the dialogue was anything but normal when Timothy brought up the subject of why he was here at SCI-Rockview.

"The state is so adamant about killing me," said the condemned man, "so I wrote a letter to the Governor and asked him to sign my death warrant. My appeals were nothing more than an opportunity for me to set the record straight—to save my own life. I have been fighting for so long, but for me there is no justice in the Pennsylvania court system . . . only political vengeance. I no longer want to sit in a cell 23 hours a day,[1] just to spend the rest of my life in misery. I am tired, and I want to die."

As a human being, I could not believe the words I was hearing. But as a correctional officer assigned to guard a Death Row convict, it was nothing more than a job. After all, the man had committed murder. Society does not easily forgive when a citizen kills one of its own.

*   *   *

Timothy told me every detail of his trip from SCI-Greene, in the southwestern part of Pennsylvania, to SCI-Rockview where he would be executed the following day. During the long trip across the hills and valleys of the great Keystone State, he looked out the van window to watch the passing scenery: the trees, the tall corn, the farm houses, the antique-styled barns, the horses and cows in the fields, the majestic ridges of the mountains in the background, and the splendid skies above. When he was a child and traveled with his parents around the state, he took all this beauty for granted. On this day, however, he appreciated it more than ever before. To him, it was a beautiful day.

He saw people in cars as they passed him on the highway. One young boy even waved at him. He smiled back but could not wave, because his hands were restrained by metal handcuffs secured to a leather belt around his waist. He imagined that the boy thought he was just another ordinary traveler. He felt the wind rustle his hair, reminded of how his mother used to run her fingers through his hair and call him her "little man." He had not seen his mother in many years, but he was sure that she was thinking about him that day.

A large Weis Markets tractor-trailer passed by. Timothy recalled being in a Weis Market when he was 6 years old, where he picked up a box of Captain Crunch cereal and asked his parents if they would buy it for him. "Put it back, now!" his father yelled.

When they drove home from the store, his dad was very angry. He had told Timothy over and over not to ask for items they could not afford. He said the only way Timothy would learn was if he beat it into him. So he beat Timothy relentlessly with his fists, until the boy lost consciousness. Timothy remembered other times when his father drank, raged, and beat him, as well as his mother. His father took off when Timothy was 7, and no one saw him ever since.

Lost in the past, Timothy quietly started to cry. The driver looked in the rear-view mirror and asked him if he was all right.

Timothy told me that when he became a young man, he did his share of drinking, drugs, and abusing girlfriends. He also committed violent crimes against innocent people. One day, he was arrested. After making bail, he killed a witness who was going to testify against him at trial. For this murder, he received the death penalty. It was the most confusing time in his life.

That was 14 years ago. Since then, he had not consumed any alcohol or drugs. At the bottom of life's ladder, he cried out for help. He began to read the Holy Scriptures and accepted Jesus Christ into his life. He received forgiveness from his Creator, loosened the bondage that trapped his soul, and changed his ways of thinking. He was now a kind and decent man, so he claimed. Somehow, I believed him.

Timothy described the end of his road trip to Rockview's infamous "farmhouse." The driver turned down a long, narrow road, and Timothy could hear the stones crunching under the tires. The van stopped at what appeared to be a barn house. The driver and guard opened the side door, and one of them said, "Okay, Timothy, we're here." Helped out of the van, Timothy paused a few seconds for one last look at the surrounding scenery. On the edge of the roof, he noticed a small, brown sparrow watching him. It was indeed a beautiful day.

*   *   *

When not occupying his time in conversation with me, Timothy usually crouched up on his bed and read his Bible. He was permitted a half-hour phone call. Although I did not intentionally eavesdrop on the conversation, I overheard him say, "Mom, I'm so sorry. . ."

As I prepared to leave my shift at 10 P.M., Timothy asked me if I considered myself a member of society. I told him that I did. He then asked me to forgive him for what he had done. "It's not my place to forgive you," I said. "But if it'll make you feel any better, I have nothing against you." Then I left for home.

*   *   *

The following morning over breakfast and newspaper, I saw that today's execution had made the front page. Much to my surprise, the victim's mother sent a letter to the Governor, pleading for him to stop the execution. For whatever reasons, these pleas fell on deaf ears, because later that afternoon I spent the last remaining hours of Timothy's life with him as he prepared to die.

*   *   *

Timothy greeted me with a smile, which I did not expect. "They're going to execute me by lethal injection," he blurted out. "They say that it's more humane than the electric chair."

How could I reply to that? It was not my job to argue for or against the death penalty, and I reminded Timothy that I was just here to do my job.

"Well, when they place the poison in my body," he continued, "isn't it a willful, premeditated, and deliberate act? Isn't society doing to me exactly what it says it condemns . . . murder? First-degree murder?"

I had to admit to myself that he was making a lot of sense, but I remained silent. I wanted to ask him why or how he could have murdered another human being, but the superintendent had warned us not to ask personal questions. In fact, we were instructed not to become too attached to Death Row prisoners. "Just try to make them as comfortable as possible," the superintendent had said. As an agent of the state, I did what the state told me to do. I must confess, though, that I felt uneasy about being a part of this process.

Other guards who volunteered to be stationed at the death house also expressed their discomfort. Some never said anything about it, yet I could sense that this was an unpleasant job for them as well. One guard was quite happy about it, however, remarking that he wished he could inject the poison himself.

* * *

I do not remember what Timothy's last meal was, but I do know that his request was accommodated. He was given the opportunity to take a shower, and I personally delivered his outgoing mail to one of the prison administrators. A chaplain came to visit him, and I watched as they prayed together. There was no doubt by the expression on the chaplain's face that he too was vexed over his participation in this event. Timothy was also allowed speak with his family during a noncontact[2] visit. I do not know who actually came to see him.

An hour before Timothy would be put to sleep, I watched him kneel on the floor of his cell next to his bed, his Bible open, praying to his Creator. Perhaps he was praying for his family, for his victim's family, for forgiveness, for peace, or whatever, but I heard him end his prayer with these words: "Forgive them, Father, for they know not what they do." That hit me hard, because I and everyone else involved in his execution knew exactly what we were doing.

* * *

The superintendent came to Timothy's cell and read him the death warrant, as though he had done it a thousand times before. From the side of the cell, I saw a stream of tears trickling down Timothy's face. Someone asked him if he was going to go peacefully without any incident, and he answered that he was ready. He was then handcuffed in front of his body, and restraints were attached from the handcuffs to the leather belt around his waist. His ankles were also shackled.

Half an hour before the scheduled execution, Timothy was escorted through a side entrance into the death chamber. Unable to mount the table, he was assisted by myself and another guard. His arms, neck, chest, and legs were then secured with restraint straps. His arms outstretched from both sides of his body reminded me of a crucifixion.

Once Timothy had been secured on the table, the doctor spoke to him in a friendly manner and explained the specific procedures of what would happen. I wanted to tell the doctor to shut up, until I realized that he too had a job to do. Timothy seemed to be relaxed. While the doctor spoke, Timothy closed his eyes in the final minutes of preparation.

Three chemicals would flow into his body, the doctor explained. The first would relax him, the second would put him to sleep, and the third would stop his heart from beating. These poisons would flow down one at a time through a hollow plastic tube inserted into his arm.

Before the doctor inserted the intravenous needle into Timothy's arm, he soaked a gauze pad with ethyl alcohol and wiped the injection area. I thought, why would they sterilize his arm if they're putting him to death? Were they afraid he would get an infection? The doctor later told me that it was simply a medical procedure. "Ethics," he said. It occurred to me that the Hippocratic Oath states that a physician must never harm a patient but do everything to preserve his life.

The curtain inside the death chamber was opened, revealing two separate rooms with observation windows. One, I believe, was for the members of the victim's family; the other for the condemned man's family and for chosen witnesses. Members of the media, selected by the superintendent, were also present.

As I looked out through the windows, I could see that some people were upset, while others sat without expression. It was clear, though, that they were disturbed by the sight of Timothy strapped down to the table as he tried to look out towards them.

He was then asked if he wanted to make a final statement. With calmness and simplicity, Timothy asked to be forgiven for what he had done. Nothing more. When he finished, the doctor told him that he may want to close his eyes. Timothy did so.

The doctor turned on a pump machine that controlled the flow of chemicals. I heard a loud click echo inside the death chamber. I looked at Timothy. His eyes were still closed. "Unto You, I commend my spirit, Father," he mumbled softly as the first fluids traveled down the tube and into his body. The doctor and I suddenly exchanged looks, then he shifted his eyes away. Within a minute or so, I could see that the first container in the machine was empty. Another echoing click. The second chemical worked its way down.

During this, Timothy was slowly but surely losing consciousness. I looked back toward the windows at the witnesses. Most had their heads lowered, but some actually kept that expressionless gaze and seemed to be watching out of curiosity. Underneath my Pennsylvania Department of Corrections uniform, I could feel my armpits perspiring, yet I was not even breathing that heavily.

The last click. The final chemical. The last moments of a human life. The last seconds. Timothy's chest appeared to heave one final time, then . . . it stopped moving. Time seemed to stand still—until the heartbeat monitor screamed, its echo reverberating inside my head.

An administrator closed the curtain, and the doctor placed his stethoscope on the body, searching for a sign of life. There was nothing, only silence. Death was a reality. The doctor looked over at the superintendent and told him that Timothy Ryan was dead, announcing the time of his expiration.

We were instructed to place his lifeless body into a thick, black plastic bag that the doctor himself closed. Once sealed inside the body bag, Timothy was then removed from the death chamber and taken to a side entrance where a vehicle waited to take him away. I watched the door slam shut and heard the stones on the ground crunching underneath the tires as it drove away, just as Timothy had described the sound when he first arrived.

After work, I went to a bar and thought about all the stories Timothy had shared with me. It seemed to me that there must be a better way to deal with those who commit acts of murder than what I had witnessed tonight.

Endnotes

1. Capital case prisoners in Pennsylvania are classified as Custody Level 5 (maximum security), which means they are confined to their cells 23 hours a day, allowing only one hour for outside exercise. See Chapter 22.
2. "Noncontact" means that some partition, such as Plexiglas, is between the prisoner and the visitors, so that they cannot touch each other. ✦

Chapter 37

A Life for a Life

> But if there is serious injury, you are to take life for a life . . . eye for eye, tooth for tooth, hand for hand, foot for foot . . . burn for burn, wound for wound, stripe for stripe.
>
> —Exodus 21:23–25, *The Book of Yahweh (Holy Scriptures)*

> An eye for an eye leaves everyone blind.
>
> —Mohandas K. Gandhi

In 1999, while incarcerated at SCI-Frackville, I read a book entitled *Life Without Parole*, written by Victor Hassine, a fellow Pennsylvania prisoner sentenced to life imprisonment. Its title caught my attention, and I wanted to hear what he had to say about Pennsylvania lifers. When I finished the book, I was disappointed. The text focused principally on the living conditions inside our state prisons and had little, if anything, to do with lifers as a particular group of inmates.

When I arrived at SCI-Rockview later that year, I read the book again, then decided to send a letter voicing my disappointment to its editor, Thomas J. Bernard, a professor at Pennsylvania State University. I also challenged him with a proposal to assist me in writing a book of my own, well aware of my inexperience in literary endeavors. The topic I had in mind? What else? Pennsylvania lifers.

I never expected to hear from him and was even more surprised when he came to visit me at the same state prison where Mr.

Hassine had written his book. Professor Bernard patiently listened to my complaints about the book's portrayal of lifers, or lack of one, then he asked me: "Can you paint a better picture?"

In essence, a painting allows one to view what an artist portrays only from a single angle. In a metaphorical sense, Professor Bernard and I searched for a large, amorphous chunk of granite. After considerable frustration, we found one and for three years chiseled away at this rock, shaping it into a form that would allow readers to view it from several different angles. We hope that this book accurately depicts a subject that has been seriously neglected by society but truly deserves more meaningful study.

* * *

My underlying motivation for writing this book is to help the reader better understand the everyday experiences and realities of Pennsylvania's penal system and how it deals with its life-sentenced prisoners.

When Pennsylvania first introduced the legal term "life imprisonment" in 1925, its precise definition was not clearly established. Even as it exists today, the legislative language that defines life imprisonment in Pennsylvania does not state whether or not the punishment itself carries the possibility of parole. Life imprisonment in this state's history, however, has always been interpreted by its judicial system as a sentence that holds no hope for parole.

Lifers are eligible to receive clemency from the Governor, by which nonparolable life imprisonment is commuted to a parolable sentence. In the 69 years between 1925 and 1994, in fact, Pennsylvania governors granted executive clemency to nearly 350 lifers.

That changed drastically in 1994, when lifer Reginald McFadden was released from prison for apparently political reasons. Subsequently, McFadden moved to New York State, where he raped and murdered innocent people. Since then, Pennsylvania's governors have denied all requests from life-sentenced inmates to commute their sentences.[1]

Life imprisonment may seem desirable to society, as well as to victims of crime, but it engenders many counterproductive results. Punishment by imprisonment only works when justice is meted out in a fashion that restores moral rightness. Excessive punishment, such as life imprisonment without parole, creates many harmful psychological and financial consequences not only for the person serving the sentence but for all those impacted by the crime, including the community at large.

Life imprisonment only serves to destroy lives and at best should be reserved solely for the most dangerous of offenders who cannot or will not be redeemed. Many lifers in Pennsylvania today are not the same individuals they once were, many of whom by their longstanding commendable performances in prison have earned at least a fighting chance for parole.

As it now stands, Pennsylvania lifers have no hope of ever being released from prison. Consequently, the state's lifer population has exploded beyond all proportion—to the point where we are now the largest population of prisoners serving life imprisonment (without parole) in the world.

A sentence of life imprisonment has become literally a "death sentence," one that society knows little or nothing about, nor cares to. In reality, the only difference between capital punishment and life imprisonment is the amount of time it takes for the prisoner to die.

*   *   *

The title of this book, as well as this chapter, is *A Life for a Life*. I took away another human being's life, and I have lost my own life as a consequence.

I was born and raised in Allentown, Pennsylvania, to parents who were great family providers. I was also blessed that they sent me to both public and private schools. Around 18 years of age, my life took a turn for the worse. My mother was diagnosed with terminal ovarian cancer. The relationship between my father and I was faltering. My only source of comfort came from a girlfriend whom I fell in love with and planned to marry. Six months before graduation, we both quit high school. In January of 1990, my fiancée and I left home and moved to Philadelphia where I secured two jobs and an apartment to support us both.

In April of that year, while drinking heavily, I seemed to have momentarily lost my mind and fired a rifle from my apartment window. Within a 22-hour period, I shot two different people, one of whom died.

Trying to fathom my incomprehensible actions, I later discovered that the medication (phenytoin) I was taking for petit mal epilepsy had interacted with the consumption of the alcohol and produced delirium. This, of course, does nothing to excuse my behavior nor change its consequences. One person's life was abruptly and tragically ended, while many other people's lives were irreparably damaged. For myself, however, I must hold onto this fact, because it helps me to understand how I could have committed such an incredibly terrible act.

Not a day goes by that I do not think about all the people who I have harmed. My crime has filled the lives of my victims' families with grief and pain, as well as those of my own family. I do not know if it will ever be possible for all of them to forgive me nor, despite my wish for forgiveness, can I ever expect it.

*   *   *

As a life-sentenced inmate, there are very few things that I can do to help other people. I can only hope and pray that this book will somehow contribute to the society that I have harmed and in which I am no longer allowed to live.

I hope too that this literary effort will bring me closer to redemption in my own life. Writing these words has been one way to help me to reclaim a portion of that life. Instead of society losing two lives because of my actions, perhaps through this book it will only lose one.

*   *   *

Since the first creation of the Pennsylvania Lifers' Association at SCI-Huntingdon in 1971, lifer organizations and their support groups from across the state have dedicated themselves to serving both prisons and outside communities. In addition to coordinating various educational programs, seminars, and workshops that promote leadership as well as rehabilitative skills, these lifer organizations coordinate fundraisers that benefit the following charities:

- Make-A-Wish Foundation, Easter Seals, American Lung Foundation, United Way, Muscular Dystrophy Association, Pennsylvania Prison Society, PA CURE, Women's Resource

Centers, Boy/Girl Scouts of America, Families of Murder Victims Program, Victim/Offender Reconciliation Program (VORP), drug treatment centers, children's hospitals, and many more!

- In 1979, the Pennsylvania Lifers' Association at SCI-Rockview coordinated the first Prison Runathon with Centre-Peace, Inc., an organization that promotes alternatives to the incarceration of our youth. The Prison Runathon is now the largest inmate philanthropic effort in the world, raising tens of thousands of dollars for Pennsylvania's Big Brothers/Big Sisters Foundation chapters annually.

- Pennsylvania lifers continue their struggle to pass legislation that would grant them parole eligibility consideration. For more information on Pennsylvania's life-sentenced prisoners, please write to the following:

> Pennsylvania Lifers' Support Group
> P.O. Box 256
> Wellsboro, PA 16901-0256

> Financial contributions can be sent to the following:

> The Lobbyist Coalition Fund
> 103 N. Main Street
> Hatfield, PA 19440-2419

- The Lobbyist Coalition is a criminal justice advocacy group formed in 1999 by four nonprofit organizations in Pennsylvania. Its general purpose is to lobby for penal and criminal justice system reform. This coalition encourages the passage of restorative-justice legislation, particularly for nonviolent prisoners, and lobbies for fair penal justice. In particular, it advocates legislation that would allow life-sentenced inmates to be considered for parole after serving 25 years.

The Lobbyist Coalition is a 501(c) nonprofit organization. All book royalties earned by the author from this book are paid directly to the Lobbyist Coalition.

Endnote

1. In 2003, days before he left office, Governor Mark Schweiker commuted the life sentence of a man who had lent a gun that was later used in a fatal bar robbery. This man claimed complete innocence but was convicted and sentenced to life imprisonment without parole. He had served 21 years at the time his sentence was commuted. In contrast, the man who had borrowed the gun from him was acquitted at trial. This was the first commutation of a life-sentenced inmate in Pennsylvania in over eight years. ✦

About the Editors

Thomas J. Bernard is Professor of Crime, Law, Justice and Sociology at Pennsylvania State University. He has published extensively on criminology theory and juvenile justice. In addition to co-editing James A. Paluch, Jr.'s *A Life for A Life*, Dr. Bernard also has co-edited Victor Hassine's *Life Without Parole*, Third Edition (Roxbury Publishing, 2003), and K. C. Carceral's *Behind a Convict's Eyes* (Wadsworth, 2003).

Robert Johnson is a Professor of Justice, Law and Society at The American University in Washington, DC. His scholarly works include *Culture and Crisis in Confinement, Condemned To Die: Life Under Sentence of Death, The Pains of Imprisonment, Hard Time: Understanding and Reforming the Prison, Death Work: A Study of the Modern Execution Process,* and *Crime and Punishment: Inside Views* (Roxbury Publishing, 2000), as well as over 30 articles published in journals and anthologies. Johnson is a faculty member (Honora Causa) of Phi Kappa Phi, and has been formally honored as a Distinguished Alumnus of the Nelson A. Rockefeller College of Public Affairs and Policy, University at Albany, State University of New York. ✦

Bibliography

Abbott, J. H. (1981). *In The Belly of the Beast*. New York: Vintage Books.

Abu-Jamal, M. (1995). *Live From Death Row*, 2nd ed. New York: Avon Books.

———. (1997). *Death Blossoms*. Pennsylvania: Plough Publishing.

Burger, J. (1995). "Accused Serial Killer And The Path To Freedom." *New York Times* (April 4).

Carpenter v. Vaughn, 296 F.3d 138 (2002).

Castle v. PA Board of Probation and Parole, 554.A.2d 625 (1989).

Cheatwood, D. (1988). "The Life-Without-Parole Sanction: Its Current Status and a Research Agenda." *Crime & Delinquency* 34 (43, 45, 48).

Commonwealth v. Aljoe, 216 A.2d 50 (1966).

Commonwealth v. Chandler, 554 Pa. 401 (1998).

Commonwealth v. Christy, 540 Pa. 192 (1995).

Commonwealth v. Clark, 551 Pa. 258, 710 A.2d 31 (1998).

Commonwealth v. Henry, 524 Pa. 135 (1990).

Commonwealth v. Johnson, 368 Pa. 139 (1951).

Commonwealth v. King, 554 Pa. 331, 721 A.2d 763 (1998).

Commonwealth v. Martin, 554 Pa. 331 (1998).

Commonwealth v. May, 551 Pa. 286 (1998).

Commonwealth v. Robinson, 554 Pa. 293, 721 A.2d 344 (1998).

Commonwealth v. Rogers, 335 Pa. Super. 130, 483 A.2d 990 (1984)

Commonwealth v. Simmons, 541 Pa. 211 (1995).

Commonwealth v. Smith, 176 A.2d 619 (1962).

Commonwealth v. Trivigno, 561 Pa. 232, 750 A.2d 243 (2000).

Commonwealth v. Wyche, 467 A.2d 636 (1983).

Commonwealth v. Zettlemoyer, 500 Pa. 16 (1982).

Conover, J. (2001). *Newjack: Guarding Sing Sing*. New York: Random House.

Gauker, J. (2000). "We Are Healthier When We Pardon." *Graterfriends* 18 (1).

Hailey, E. F. (1987). *Life Sentence.* New York: Dell.

Hassine V. (1999). *Life Without Parole,* 2nd ed. Los Angeles: Roxbury.

Herrick, D. (1998). "Lifers Eligible For Parole In Most States." *Corrections Compendium* (May).

Keedy, E. R. (1949). "History of the Pennsylvania Statute Creating Degrees of Murder." *University of Pennsylvania Law Review* 97 (759).

Kroll, M. A. (1989). *Facing the Death Penalty: Essays on a Cruel and Unusual Punishment.* Pennsylvania: Temple University Press.

Langer, S. (1979). *The Rahway State Prison Lifers' Group.* Union, NJ: Department of Sociology and Social Work, Kean College of New Jersey.

Martin, A. W. (1985). *Caesar's Gladiator Pit.* Pennsylvania: Tower Press.

Meyers v. Gillis, 142 F.3d 138 (1998).

Nelson, R. (1993). *Life Sentences.* New York: Faber & Faber.

Paduano, A., and Smith, C. (1987). "Deadly Errors: Juror Misperceptions Concerning Parole in the Imposition of the Death Penalty." *Colum. Human Rights Law Review* 211 (222–225).

Paluch, Jr., J. A. (1995). "Life In Pennsylvania Means Just That . . . Life!" *Prison News Service* (Fall).

Perske, R. (1991). *Unequal Justice?* Tennessee: Abingdon Press.

Prejean, H. (1992). *Dead Man Walking.* New York: Random House.

Prell, L. E. (1985). *Iowa Inmates Sentenced to Life Terms: A Survey of Class A Felons.* Des Moines, IA: Iowa Department of Human Rights.

Reed, J. R. (1996). *Life Sentences.* Detroit, MI: Wayne State University Press.

Renninger, P. (1982). *A Study of Recidivism Among Individuals Granted Executive Clemency in Pennsylvania: 1968–1981.* Pennsylvania: PA Commission On Crime and Delinquency, May 25.

Rideau, W., and Wikberg, R. (1992). *Life Sentences: Rage and Survival, Behind Bars.* New York: Times Books, a division of Random House.

Rowan, M., and Kane, B. S. (1992). "Life Means Life, Maybe? An Analysis of Pennsylvania's Policy Toward Lifers." *Duquense Law Review* 30 (661).

Sapsford, R. (1983). *Life Sentence Prisoners.* Pennsylvania: Open University Press.

Scarbrough v. Johnson, 300 F.3d 302 (2002). See dissenting opinion.

Senate Bill 313. *Pennsylvania Legislative Journal,* December 27, 1965.

Simmons v. South Carolina, 114 S.Ct. 2187, 512 U.S. 154 (1994).

Weiss, K. (1976). *The Prison Experience: An Anthology.* New York: Delacorte.

Wenger v. Frank, 266 F.3d 218 (2001).

Williams, S. T. (2001). *Life in Prison.* Madison, WI: Turtleback.

Wright, Jr., J. H. (1990). "Life-Without-Parole: An Alternative to Death or not Much of a Life at All?" *Vanderbilt Law Review* 529.

Zehr, H. (1990). *Changing Lenses.* Pennsylvania: Herald Press.

———. (1996). *Doing Life: Reflections of Men and Women Serving Life Sentences.* Pennsylvania: Good Books. ✦